# Spirit of Harlem

DOUBLEDAY

New York

London   Toronto   Sydney

Auckland

# Spirit

## of

# Harlem

A Portrait of America's
Most Exciting Neighborhood

CRAIG MARBERRY
AND
MICHAEL CUNNINGHAM

Foreword by Gordon Parks

PUBLISHED BY DOUBLEDAY
a division of Random House, Inc.

DOUBLEDAY and the portrayal of an anchor with a dolphin are
registered trademarks of Random House, Inc.

Library of Congress Cataloging-in-Publication Data
Marberry, Craig.
Spirit of Harlem, a portrait of America's most exciting neighborhood /
Craig Marberry and Michael Cunningham.—1st ed.
p.   cm.
1. Harlem (New York, N.Y.)—Social life and customs—Pictorial works.  2. Harlem (New
York, N.Y.)—Social life and customs—Anecdotes.  3. Harlem (New York,
N.Y.)—Biography.  4. African Americans—New York (State)—New York—Social life and
customs—Pictorial works  5. African Americans—New York (State)—New York—Social life
and customs—Anecdotes.  6. African Americans—New York (State)—New
York—Interviews.  7. New York (N.Y.)—Social life and customs—Pictorial works.
8. New York (N.Y.)—Social life and customs—Anecdotes.  9. New York (N.Y.)—Biography.
I. Cunningham, Michael, 1969 Feb. 27–   II. Title.
F128.68.H3M29  2003
974.7'1—dc21       2003043968

ISBN 0-385-50406-3

PRINTED IN THE UNITED STATES OF AMERICA

December 2003
First Edition

1   3   5   7   9   10   8   6   4   2

In memory of Craig's beloved grandmother,
Margaret Little Ford,
and to Michael's father,
Dennis Cunningham Sr.

# Foreword

There are places I've seen, and there are places I've known. Harlem, I'm grateful to say, is a place I've known. I was born in the small prairie town of Fort Scott, Kansas, but over the decades Harlem has fed my belly and my soul. Even when I turned the camera and the pen on Harlem to report ugly truths, it nonetheless smiled on me.

Since I first chronicled Harlem for *Life* magazine in 1948, the years have fallen hurriedly as autumn leaves. Harlem, despite the passage of time, is still generous to outsiders like me. I know this because it has smiled on author Craig Marberry and photographer Michael Cunningham, who live in North Carolina and Washington, D.C., respectively. Their collection of narratives and photographs plunges deep into the heart of Harlem, sometimes discovering sunken treasure, sometimes the scattered remnants of dreams broken. What they bring to the surface is something precious and real about a place that has long bewitched the world. Their work humanizes this sanguine time in Harlem's evolution.

The book sprouted from Marberry's enduring fascination with Harlem, which he first visited as a boy. For a year before he found a publisher, Marberry made frequent visits to Harlem. He came to interview potential subjects, but he also came to feed the hunger of his inquisitiveness, to get a clear view of the mythical neighborhood that he had only squinted at from afar.

What he discovered was a Harlem in the midst of change, a flux of economic and cultural resurgence into an ocean of poverty and decay. After a seemingly bottomless decline, an economic revival has come to Harlem, though the most deprived and destitute watch from outside the tent. Consequently, Marberry found physicians and drug addicts, scholars and the unschooled, home owners and residents of public housing, eager newcomers and embittered old-timers. He found them by exploring Harlem, and not from the sterile distance of a taxi or tour bus. He explored the old-fashioned way: He beat the streets. He walked. His scouting brings to mind words from a poem by a lion of the Harlem Renaissance, Claude McKay:

> *Ah, heart of me, the weary, weary feet*
> *In Harlem wandering from street to street.*

The weary feet in McKay's poem belong to a prostitute. Marberry must surely empathize, having solicited more than a hundred interviews while working on the book.

When Cunningham joined the project, he too did some stepping. Marberry introduced Cunningham to James Ford, a fifty-five-year-old Harlem native who was one of the first to be interviewed. Ford volunteered to escort Cunningham around his beloved neighborhood, helping open his shutter to an insider's Harlem. That tour lasted for hours.

In Harlem, photographers are plentiful as brownstones. But few aspire to produce the sort of images Cunningham has created. These photographs convey a sense of place and identity. Whether it's Olympic fencer Akhnaten Spencer-EL looking not at all out of place as he poses with his saber and mask on a train platform on 125th Street, or whether it's bookstore owner Clara Villarosa having a "good read" on a bench at the Harlem Meer, this is a timely pictorial history.

Likewise, Marberry renders revealing interviews. They peel away shrouds and masks to expose authentic faces, voices free of reticence or pretense, even when describing subjects unpleasant. A hair braider from Senegal, for instance, laments the arduous life of West African immigrants who work under poor conditions because shop owners say "they live like animals in the jungle back home, so put them in a little, dirty room." Conversely, some narratives amuse, like the one about an elderly couple who run a funeral home in their Victorian house, built in 1888 by "the king of circus men," James Bailey of Barnum and Bailey. The couple have a china cabinet crammed with cremation urns dating back to 1954. Superstitious families leave urns behind because they "don't want to wake up in the middle of the night and find uncle so-and-so hovering over [them]."

Peruse the pages of this collaboration and you'll glimpse the vivid soul of Harlem, light refracted into a rainbow of colors. I found some old friends, to boot. I first met Evelyn Cunningham, the legendary Harlem journalist, some forty years ago in the lobby of the Hotel Theresa, long before "the Waldorf of Harlem" was converted into an office building, long before our blossomed peaks were capped with snow. Marvin Smith and I go way back, too. He and his late twin, Morgan, practiced photographic journalism in Harlem nearly a decade and a half before my first assignment there. The twins opened their arms to me with altruism not shown them by a Harlem landlord, who once refused to rent them a street-level space for their studio because of the color of their skin. Black businesses were relegated to upper floors. "That's how it was on 125th Street," says Marvin. "That's how it was in Harlem."

Harlem is a place I have known. No matter how well you think you know Harlem, however, it can glint a new facet and surprise you.

GORDON PARKS

# Author's Note

My first taste of Harlem came at age eleven, when my mother took my four brothers and me to New York on summer vacation. With wide eyes, we visited the obligatory sites downtown, from the Empire State Building to the United Nations. Then, one afternoon, Mom took us up to Harlem, and suddenly the Emerald City felt more like the south side of Chicago, more like home. The place looked nothing like our neighborhood, with its dilapidated brownstones, lined up shoulder to shoulder like combat-weary soldiers, instead of charming single-family homes; and its stoops that descended into slabs of concrete instead of manicured lawns. Yet, along Harlem's cluttered side streets, I heard voices I might know. Along Harlem's canyon-wide boulevards, I saw faces I might recognize.

But what I remember most about that excursion uptown was our meal at Sylvia's Restaurant. I can still taste the corn bread, collards, candied yams, and fried pork chops, all so faithful to my grandmother's own. (My grandmother, like restaurateur Sylvia Woods, grew up in South Carolina.) And I can hear the babble, happy babble, that swirled through the restaurant like the aroma of sweet potato pie, hot from the oven, voices wafting as they did Sunday afternoons in the dining hall of my grandfather's church.

Harlem, in the same breath, was both alien and immediately familiar.

It would be another dozen years, however, before I would get better acquainted with Harlem, while studying journalism at nearby Columbia University. Back then, Harlem had a menacing reputation. University officials warned students to keep out for our own safety. I ignored them. Harlem was where I went for haircuts, for freelance work, for an occasional taste of home at Sylvia's.

Any visitor soon discovers that Harlem is more than a place. It is a people. Some—like choreographer Robert Garland of the Dance Theatre of Harlem—are eminent in their fields. But most are everyday people with stories to tell. As a student, I felt drawn to those stories, overheard from barber's chairs and church pews and crowded lunch counters. People talked about Harlem's days in the sun, about long hours and hard times, about a song on the radio—a golden flash from their past—sung so sweet.

It was those stories, those voices, that I had in mind when I began working on this project in July of 2000. I envisioned the book as an intimate stroll through the world's most famous neighborhood. In other words, if you walked the streets of Harlem, then these would be the diverse people you might meet, the captivating tales you might hear. Some would reflect on Harlem's glory days with merriment; others would open a window to life in a Harlem that had long ago lost its luster, the terrible sadness of ruination. Some would muse on Harlem's promise; others would recount the intriguing circumstances that led them there, drew them with the resolve of migratory birds.

And so I strolled.

My feet led me first to the Abraham Lincoln projects. I was surprised to discover there a dozen or so men playing chess near the intersection of 135th and Fifth Avenue, known to Harlem's chess enthusiasts as The Corner. Among the no-nonsense competitors was Gregory Civers, a streetwise fifteen year old who began learning the game on The Corner at age five—which explains why, to his embarrassment, he sometimes calls a "knight" a "horsey." (Civers is the youngest person featured in the book. The most senior is the irrepressible then ninety-three-year-old Isabel Powell, a former dancer at the legendary Cotton Club and first wife of renowned Harlem pastor and Congressman Adam Clayton Powell Jr. "When Adam graduated from Colgate University," Isabel Powell said, "[his father] put him on a ship and sent him to Europe. . . . He wanted to make Adam forget me. But there was no forgetting *me*.")

Later that first day, I walked past a row of murals, stunning portraits of local residents rendered with, it appeared, thousands of colorful brush strokes. Up close, the strokes were as disintegrated as confetti. But from a distance magic happened. The confetti came alive. It meshed to form knowing eyes or untroubled grins or graying heads held high. It breathed life and pride into the anonymous faces of Harlem. The murals were affixed to an abandoned building, clashing like fresh boutonnieres on a ragged suit. I looked for the artist's name on the murals but, to my disappointment, they were unsigned. When I later interviewed the artist, Brett Cook-Dizney, he explained—to my astonishment—that he created the intricate works not with a brush, but with cans of spray paint. "Why don't you sign your paintings?" I asked. "It's not about me," he said. "It's about the work. It's about Harlem."

Next, my feet took me to Memorial Baptist Church, where I heard gospel singer Alice McClarty rattle the stained glass with her rendition of "He's Sweet I Know." During that visit, it was Deacon James Ford who opened my eyes to the popularity of gospel in Harlem. Each week, he explained, thousands of tourists from Europe and Asia flock to Harlem churches to hear the spirited music. "I call this reverse missionary work," said Deacon Ford. "Instead of us going out to foreign lands, they come to us."

Historians say people have been flocking to Harlem for centuries. Enticed by its fertile farmland—long inhabited by Native Americans—the Dutch "settled" Nieuw Haarlem, with slave labor, in 1658. By the eighteenth century, Harlem was also a summer retreat for Lower Manhattan's well heeled, who erected stately manors like the Morris-Jumel Mansion, which still stands. (The mansion served as temporary headquarters for George Washington during the Revolutionary War.) The arrival of elevated trains in the late 1870s sparked the development of some of Harlem's most resplendent neighborhoods. But fifteen years later, the building boom went bust in the midst of an economic depression, and developers began erecting five-story tenements, populated mainly by immigrant Italians and Jews. Landlords would not rent to black families until the early 1900s, when African-American real estate agent Philip A. Payton persuaded a handful of landlords to reconsider. Soon thereafter, as large numbers of blacks arrived from Southern states, from the Caribbean, and from overcrowded downtown communities, whites began to flee Harlem. In the mid-1920s through the Great Depression of 1929, the period of the legendary Harlem Renaissance, the community became known as the cultural capital of black America. During the depression, however, many black middle-class residents abandoned Harlem, and it began to erode. Eventually, failing schools, fractured families, and rampant crime became synonymous with Harlem. Latinos then West Africans immigrated in eager droves, but the glory days seemed not only gone, but forever lost.

But Harlem is again found, as far as public and private investment are concerned. Soaring rents downtown spurred a run on Harlem properties, which are being restored and renovated. Lured by tax incentives, major corporate chains such as Blockbuster and Old Navy have opened stores in Harlem. And former president Bill Clinton brought worldwide attention to Harlem's decade-old economic rebound when he located his office on 125th Street in July of 2001. Detractors, however, question the merit of Harlem's latest metamorphosis, this so-called Second Renaissance. They fear that the turnabout will displace longtime residents and endanger the community's cultural heritage.

You'll find stories about that controversy within these pages. But, mostly, you'll find a Harlem that may surprise you—stories like the one from Dr. Charles Felton, who was the first to examine Dr. Martin Luther King Jr. when he was rushed to Harlem Hospital after a deranged woman stabbed him in the chest with a letter opener. As Dr. Felton recalled, "The letter opener shook every time his heart beat."

Some stories underscore Harlem's cultural vitality, giving you a seat on the sidelines of a basketball court where some say NBA-style ball was born, a seat on a church pew where a Japanese woman sings gospel music with an endearing accent, and a seat on the hood of a car whose radio blasts a song that jolts four boys on 125th Street into doing the Harlem Shake, a hip-hop dance that, according to thirty-six-year-old Kevin Taylor, "only kids can do because it requires no vertebrae."

There are stories about neighborhoods: El Barrio, Strivers Row, and once-exclusive Sugar Hill, where then eighty-two-year-old Dena Hill Morrison is a longtime resident. Morrison is a former Thursday Girl, as Harlem housekeepers were dubbed back in the day because that was their day off. "It was so expensive to live on Sugar Hill," said Morrison, "that people said we ate corn flakes to pay the rent."

And, yes, some stories give a voice to drug addiction, AIDS, homelessness, and crime. Elsie Simmons, for instance, recalls her shock after discovering that a troubled teen, who was enrolled in her skills-training institute, had been abandoned to the streets by his mother when he was eight years old. Simmons asked him how he survived. He said, "I killed people. For money."

A year after I began my research and interviews, I invited photographer Michael Cunningham aboard. Based on the award-winning skill he brought to our first collaboration, *Crowns: Portraits of Black Women in Church Hats*, I was confident that he would create a memorable collection of portraits.

———

Harlem will not be ignored. No matter what you think of the place, you do think of it. You may think of Harlem as the embodiment of everything frightful about urban decay. Or you may think of Harlem as the artistic stomping grounds of big-shoed legends: entertainers Florence Mills and Duke Ellington, painters Aaron Douglas and Bruce Nugent, writers Langston Hughes and Zora Neale Hurston—the pillars of the Harlem Renaissance. But the people featured in this book think of Harlem as something very different. Something more hushed. Something more grand. Harlem, to them, is simply the multifarious community in which they work or live. It is that Harlem, the one experienced by those who know it best, that I hoped to capture in these pages, because when you explore that Harlem you discover something about us all, something lovely and something unsettling. You discover something true.

Life has a way of coming full circle in Harlem. After I interviewed saxophonist Lonnie Youngblood, he invited me to dinner at Sylvia's, where he performs gospel music during Sunday brunches. Sylvia Woods herself was kind enough to stop by our table, and graciously accepted my offer to be profiled in the book. "Have you looked at the menu yet?" she asked as she stood to leave. "No, ma'am," I said. "But I already know what I want."

I ordered the meal I first ate there three decades earlier: corn bread, collards, candied yams, and fried pork chops.

CRAIG MARBERRY

# Photographer's Note

Harlem, New York . . . I'd read about it and I'd seen photographs of the historic place that was once home to giants like Langston Hughes, Thurgood Marshall, and Duke Ellington but also to crime, poverty, and drugs. Harlem. The "Black Mecca." The fabled Harlem of the '20s, '30s, '40s, where mothers gave birth to jazz greats, poets, scholars, and gang leaders.

But who are the people who make up Harlem today? Through my camera's lens, I've attempted to capture the unique mix of contemporary Harlem: the skin tones, passions, lifestyles, and rhythms of people who unknowingly are trying to live up to the challenge of Harlem's past, *the spirit of Harlem*. In most cases, coauthor Craig Marberry interviewed our subjects before I took their portraits. I'd read his narratives and try to marry the images to the person and their story. But what an undertaking! How does one capture the richness and complexity of these individuals? My only hope is that the reader will look at the photos and read the essays and take away the spirit and feeling of Harlem.

There are a few things that I'll always remember about Harlem and its people. I enjoyed eating fish at Majester's and having breakfast at Amy Ruth's. I loved taking the number 2 subway train uptown to 125th Street and Lenox Avenue and spending time at House's Barbershop where I'd listen to the seasoned older cats toss around names like Sugar Ray Robinson and Adam Clayton Powell. At a drug rehabilitation center, James Allen sang "Straighten Up and Fly Right" and played his guitar for me as I set up my lights for his photo shoot. I was filled with awe and reverence for the generations of families who stopped by to say hello to Dr. Felton—most of whom he'd brought into the world. I got a glimpse into the strong community that is Harlem. Isabel Powell, the first wife of Adam Clayton Powell Jr., invited me back to her home after our photo shoot for relaxing dinner and conversation, and I can still taste the cool peach nectar I sipped on a hot summer morning at Lana Turner's home atop the infamous Sugar Hill. I will never forget that I was in Harlem on the morning of September 11th, during the terrorist attacks, photographing the young Olympic fencer [Akhnaten Spencer-EL]. The whole city had come to a standstill before I knew what was going on. As it turns out, the subway train in the background of the photo was the last one to leave the station before all public transportation was suspended.

To all the people I photographed for this book, thank you. You have enriched my life's journey with your time, conversation, and your beautiful faces.

MICHAEL CUNNINGHAM

# Acknowledgments

My endless gratitude to so many: Roy Ackland, Michael Henry Adams, Toya Algarin, Jala Anderson, Nigel Alston, Helena Andrews, Cecile Armstrong, Marsha Askins, Louise Baker, Ann Barnes, Betty Baye, Dan Bauer, Jo Ann Baylor, Erich Blengini, Stephanie Bourland, Rita Braver, Sheila Bridges, Ruth Brown, Alan Calhoun, Fabio Camara, Roosevelt Cartwright, Margaret Civers, Oliver Conner, Nia Damali, Cherrye Davis, Emma Davis, Giselle Davis, Martha Washington Davis, Wayne Dawkins, Chuck Deggans, Danielle DeStephan, Beth Dickey, Deirdre Donahue, Simon Doonan, Sabada Dube, Cindy Farmer, Denise Franklin, Janice Gaston, Prentis Sonny Gibbs, Thelma Golden, Naomi Graham, Phillip Gray, James Green, Bantor Gweye, Mamadou Gweye, Brian Hill, Cathy Gant Hill, Charles Hewey, Beth Hopkins, Cathy Howell, Larry G. Earl Jr., Dr. Elwanda Ingram, John Isaacs, Mara Isaacs, Sandra Jackson, Mary Jamis, Sophia Johnson, L. Scott Knackstedt, Niki Loomis, D'jean Love, Pam McDonough, Chris McElroen, Kevin McFadden, Jerry MacFarland, Johnnie McNair, Kelly Lucas, Neill McNeill, Emily Mann, Dana Marberry, Ed Marrero, Janice Marshall, Norma Martin, Dorothy Mayhew, Jane Alex Mendelson, Stephin Merritt, Toni Mosely, Edson Murray, Denise Nelson Nash, Jacob Newfeld, Wendy Newfeld, Valerie Nicholas, Alice Otchere, Frank Otchere, Kevin Praillo, Nadja Payne, Kevin Powell, Preston Powell, Barbara Quashie, Sheree Rainbow, Wilma Hill Render, Alison Rich, Gigi Roane, Arthur Rosen, Susan Rosen, Sharon Roth, Joan Rutledge, Hugh Ryan, Diegnaba Sall, Barbara Samuels, Emily Senatus, Dot Siler, April Silver, Lowery Sims, Aissatou Spencer-EL, Roberta Spivak, Wanda Starke, Starr, Dr. Delores Stephens, Carolyn Stetson, Cassandra Suggs, Belinda Tate, Regina Taylor, Beatrice Thompson, Lana Turner, Vivian L. Turner, Shirley Ullah, Linda Verdon, Renelda Walker, Chuck Wallington,

Bishop Preston Washington, Rev. Renée Washington, Steve Watson, David Weatherly, Kim White, LaVon Stennis Williams, Daryl Winfree, Lucille Hill Woodfork, Crizette Woods, Kenneth Woods, Robert Youdleman, Samara Yuvof.

Special thanks to Paula Robinson and Michele Nayman, priceless friends who were the first to critique the narratives. To the resourceful James Ford, whose tongue is incapable of speaking the word "no." To Victoria Sanders and her talented team. To our sage and tireless editor at Doubleday, Janet Hill. Working with you is such a blessing. And to the incomparable Gordon Parks for reaching back.

CRAIG MARBERRY

I would like to thank GOD, from whom all blessings flow. Thanks to Ann Barnes, Charlita Cardwell, Shereen Miller, James Ford, Janet Hill/Doubleday, Victoria Sanders and Associates, Ann Jardine, and Gordon Parks, who has influenced my life immeasurably. Special thanks to the wonderful Tycely Williams, my parents, Dennis and Patricia Cunningham, Sherrie Wallington, Camille Roddy, Raymond Jones, Derek and Tonya Caldwell, Mike and Debra Pitt, Simone Rose, and a host of others too numerous to name, thank you for your support and encouraging words over the course of this project. To Craig Marberry, a talented soul, thanks for yet another great collaboration. And to my daughter Kamari, Daddy loves you!

MICHAEL CUNNINGHAM

I, Harlem.

Island within an Island, but not

alone.

LANGSTON HUGHES

The minute you step out your door, everything

in Harlem is in your face.

There's a beauty and a poetry in all that.

LANA TURNER

# Lana Turner, 51

REAL ESTATE BROKER

In Harlem, everything is in your face. It's a man blowing a trumpet on a subway platform or a stranger asking for a dollar. It's half a dozen African women sitting on chairs along the sidewalk, asking to braid your hair. It's a kid with his shirt open and his pants falling down, moving to the music in his head. It's walking past a group of men and one of them says, "Baby, you sho' look good today." The minute you step out your door, everything in Harlem is in your face. There's a beauty and a poetry in all of that.

Some people say, "Oh, the crowded streets and the noise! How can you take it?" To me, the idea of living anywhere else is so foreign because there's so much going on here that's beautiful, that's thought provoking, that's humorous. Despite all the things we have to plow through, blacks in Harlem still have a sense of humor.

There used to be a handwritten sign on a building on Lenox Avenue, across the street from Sylvia's Restaurant. It said: "This is the future home of the Crossroads Baptist Church, whenever we can raise the money." I loved that sign. It was hilarious, and yet it said something about faith.

I think it's important to walk the streets of Harlem. You can't *feel* Harlem if you're driving by. But if you walk, you'll see all kinds of things. There's an artist by the name of David Hammons. Back when there was an empty lot filled with tall weeds next to the Studio Museum, David Hammons collected dozens and dozens of wine bottles, the cheap ones made from green glass. He took those bottles and turned them upside down and stuck them on top of the weeds. One day I was walking past the museum, not paying any attention, and was dumbfounded when I saw what he did. It was like a field of glass flowers. That to me is extraordinary. It's extraordinary because there's humor in it and there's truth in it. It said something about the larger society seeing Harlem as a throw-away society, and how Harlem, nevertheless, can see the beauty in itself, can find art in weeds and empty bottles. There's beauty in the discarded. I'll never forget that.

I don't mean to idealize Harlem. There are some things that certainly need to change. No one would say they want crime or dirty streets, and everybody wants a better education for their children. But there are many things here that are so wonderful.

There's a woman I've seen who wears a tiara every day, and some sort of fairy-tale dress. It would be easy to write her off, but there's a certain courage rooted in her attire. This is a woman who sees herself as royalty. Her statement is to herself, and she's true to it every day. Some people fashion a way to be uniquely themselves outside of what everyone else thinks. They are the mavericks who influence the music we hear, the books we read, the art we appreciate.

Yes, Harlem has its own mythic proportions attached to it, but it's not unlike other black communities throughout the United States. There's humor, there's courage, there's art. Everyone worries about, "Oh, Harlem is becoming this or that!" I don't worry. What really makes Harlem Harlem, is the soul of the place. And despite all the change coming, I don't think you can obliterate that.

If you look back to to the early 1900s,

when African Americans first came to Harlem in sizable numbers,

there were headlines in the papers that were written

in terms of a war being waged: "The Negroes Are a Menace" or,

"Negroes Take Yet Another Building on 139th Street."

MICHAEL HENRY ADAMS

# Michael Henry Adams, 45

### HISTORIAN AND AUTHOR

Once, I was conducting a tour of Harlem for the Lesbian–Gay Community Center. We were standing on Seventh Avenue and I was talking about the building across the street, and how Josephine Baker had lived there with a group of women when she was a chorus girl in Eubie Blake's musical Shuffle Along. As I was speaking, whizzing out of an upper window in the building behind us came a soda bottle. It hit a man in the head. The bottle broke and blood streamed down the man's face. Someone took him to Harlem Hospital, and four people on the tour decided they were leaving. Another man said, "Let's just cut our losses and go to lunch." I said, "No. Harlem is my home. I can't just surrender the streets to hoodlums." A woman in the group agreed, "Yeah, that's right! Let's get reinforcements and go through the building and find the person who threw the bottle." I said, "Well, I don't know about all of *that*." Anyhow, we continued the tour.

This whole notion of who belongs in Harlem, and who doesn't, is momentous. Black people here are really embittered by the prospect of displacement. You can ride on the subway and hear young men discussing what they see as white people coming and taking over Harlem. I've heard people complain about the national chains getting tax incentives to come here: the Gap, the Disney Store, Starbucks—heaven knows Manhattan doesn't need another Starbucks. And when I take tour groups around, which are often all white or predominantly white, invariably there will be a gesture of resentment toward the group. Some residents, rather than walking around the group, will very loudly and curtly say, "Excuse me!" Then they'll march through the middle of the group, the inference being, "This is *my* sidewalk. How dare you inconvenience me!"

That happens all the time. I was giving a tour last year and someone walked by and started shouting, "You people should go back where you came from. Harlem is not for sale! Harlem is not for sale!" The tragedy is that *everything* is *always* for sale. And the tragedy as far as African Americans are concerned is that we own so little of anything anywhere, including here in Harlem. A lot of people say this is our fault because we didn't buy buildings when we had the opportunity. There's something to be said for that. But as a historian, it occurs to me that this has happened before.

If you look back to the early 1900s, when African Americans first came to Harlem in sizable numbers, there were headlines in the papers that were written in terms of a war being waged: "The Negroes Are a Menace," or, "Negroes Take Yet Another Building on 139th Street." You'd think that was motivated out of pure racism, but now, as I experience the discomfiture of seeing the complexion of Harlem change, I realize that part of what those people were feeling was a sense of loss, a sense that a place they thought of as uniquely their own, a place connected to their culture and heritage, was turning into something else, was becoming someone else's.

During a recent television interview on CBS's "Sunday Morning," I said, "More and more, as I walk around Harlem, I see people who don't look like me, but who obviously live here." This was a joke to some of my white friends. They said, "What do you mean they don't look like you? They don't wear a straw hat?" But it's a concern to me because I wonder, in the wake of this change, if the African-American cultural capital can endure.

Bubba and me thought Harlem was heaven,

all the tall buildings and the lights and the sights.

One thing that stood out to me was

seeing so many black people. I asked my aunt,

"Where do the white folks live?"


REV. BETTY NEAL

# Rev. Betty Neal, *70*

### MINISTER AND ACTIVIST

I was twelve years old when they had that big riot in Harlem in 1943. I was in New York for the first time, on vacation, me and my brother, Alexander. We called him Bubba. Bubba was a year younger than me. My folks had sent us to visit with our aunt. We lived in Sumter, South Carolina, the Gamecock City, home of Revolutionary War general Thomas Sumter. There were no other houses out where we lived. We were *way* out in the woods. There was no running water, no electricity. We had a pump and kerosene lamps.

Me and Bubba were so happy about going to Harlem. Daddy took us to the bus depot. He went up to some black folk and asked who was going to New York. Somebody spoke up and Daddy asked them to watch over us. People were different in those days. You could trust strangers with your children, traveling eight hundred miles. Daddy told us to be good.

All the white people got on the bus first. When they got seated, all the black people got on and sat in the back. That's how it was.

In those days, buses didn't have toilets so they had to stop frequently. When we got off, we'd have to go on the colored folks' side of the depot to get a sandwich or anything. At one place we stopped, everybody got off except me and Bubba. We decided to sit on the front seat and open up the lunch mama made for us. Two white women had been sitting on that seat. When the driver got back on he said, "Now y'all chillins gotta go to the back of the bus. We ain't in New Yawk *yet*."

Aunt Roxanna met us at the bus station. Bubba and me thought Harlem was heaven, all the tall buildings and the lights and the sights. One thing that stood out to me was seeing so many black people. I asked my aunt, "Where do the white folks live?" She just laughed.

Aunt Roxanna lived at 239 West 116th Street. Right on the first floor. Beautiful apartment she had. She flicked a switch and a light came on. It was like a miracle. Aunt Roxanna had running water, a real bathtub. At home, we bathed in a big washtub. You had to heat the water in the fireplace or on the stove, if Mama was cooking. In the winter, the tub was in your bedroom. In the summer, it was on the back porch and you'd use cold water. At Aunt Roxanna's, I took a bath two or three times a day.

One night, the radio said there was a riot going on in Harlem. They were telling everybody to get off the street. A cop had beat up a black soldier, or shot a black soldier, and all hell broke loose. Four or five people got killed. My aunt said, "Oh, my Lord! Where's Bubba?" She ran from door to door and street to street but we couldn't find him. She said it wasn't no need calling the police because the police were busy with the riot.

Must have been around ten or eleven before Bubba came back. He said he was up on 125th watching the whole thing. He said, "Yeah, they were breaking out store windows and stealing things. People were running *everywhere*." Aunt Roxanna said, "Bubba, it's a wonder you didn't get killed."

That was *some* summer vacation.

When I was fifteen, I became a graffiti artist.

I just got cans of spray paint and went out in the middle of

the night and started doing it. . . . I was creating art

on private property so it was vandalism, but I called it

noncommissional work.

BRETT COOK-DIZNEY

# Brett Cook-Dizney, *33*

### ARTIST

My father doesn't talk to me. He's a retired educator, former assistant superintendent of schools in Oakland, California, where I grew up. His perspective is: "You have a degree in art. You have a degree in education. You could do *anything*, but you're living in an abandoned building, with no health care. How can you go to an institution like Berkeley and be satisfied living that spartan existence?"

Right before I moved to Harlem in 1997, I lived in an abandoned building in Newark, New Jersey. There was no heat. I ate potatoes every day. It was a huge building. It covered a whole block. Some nights, I could hear people breaking into the building to use drugs. I told myself, *This sacrifice will matter one day.* I've been through a lot to get here, to be an artist in Harlem.

I always loved creating art. My mother kept me quiet in church by giving me her deposit slips to draw on. When I was fifteen, I became a graffiti artist. I just got cans of spray paint and went out in the middle of the night and started doing it. That's not the traditional apprenticeship structure in graffiti, where someone usually shows you technique and style and then you fill in their lines for a while. Other graffiti artists were painting text, but I would paint figures, people in suits and fat shoestrings. I was creating art on private property so it was vandalism, but I called it noncommissional work.

People look at my murals and assume that I use brushes. But I work out of cans. Traditional painters say, "What you're doing with tone and color is incredible." Graffiti artists say, "Your can control is off the meter." Graffiti artists may not understand tone and color, but they understand how difficult it is to do what I do. When you work out of the can, you can't mix your colors on a palate. I have to do all these juxtapositions of colors to create depth and light and shadows.

I always thought graffiti was a real medium, even though the art world kicks it to the curb. But people don't know how to define what I do. Is it hip-hop? Is it high art? Is it urban beautification? Is it social activism? It's all of that, and a bunch of other stuff.

I've done thirty-something paintings here in Harlem in the last four years. *Big* eight-feet by twelve-feet panels of ordinary people who live in Harlem, people that look like your best friend's uncle on his mother's side, people you wouldn't otherwise hear about unless it was in an obituary. I hang the pieces in the neighborhoods where the subjects live. Six hundred people may come to a gallery, but if I put it outside, six hundred thousand people might see it in a day. The pieces are not going to live forever outside, but what they represent is timeless.

I never sign my work so it's difficult to get feedback. People can't find me. But that's fine because it's not about me. It's about the work. It's about Harlem. One day, as I was hanging some pieces on buildings, there was such an outpouring of gratitude. People kept coming up saying, "Thank you. Thank you." At every site, people upon people upon people. "We really appreciate this. Pictures of ourselves in Harlem. Thank you." It was one of the most profound days I've ever had as an artist. I'd like my father to understand how I felt that day, but it's a lot bigger than my father. It's about having *people* understand. Life is more than the pursuit of comfort. Life is learning to sacrifice.

I asked the counselor at our recovery program to

sit with me when I told Boo I had the virus.

Boo was so angry at me. He started yelling, "Oh, man!

You did this to *me*? My life is *over*."

LINDA HAMPTON

# Linda Hampton, *53*

## ACUPUNCTURIST

I started drinking at age eleven. When I went to P.S. 165, me, Lavern, Carol, and Nadine, we would buy wine every Thursday. We got the money from white girls who went to the Catholic school on 108th Street. Thursday was the day we went to the Catholic school for religious instruction. We'd learn how to pray, we'd learn the rosary. Didn't matter if you were Catholic or not. The class started at one o'clock so during lunch we'd circle two girls and say, "Give us your lunch money." Most of them gave it up, but some of them would fight. They had heart. But we always got the money. We'd split it up, go to this little restaurant and buy a slice of pizza, play the jukebox, and dance. We'd chip in and get our little wine, Thunderbird. Winos would buy it for us. We'd stop one and say, "Could you get this for my mother? She can't leave her bed." We'd give him the change. After all the dirt we did, we'd go to that religious-instruction class and try to get forgiveness.

I lived at 119th Street and Fifth Avenue. There were ten of us, five boys and five girls. My father wasn't really around much—just long enough to make a baby, I guess. My mother was like a Gypsy. She didn't stay anywhere too long. When I was thirteen, my mother moved to Brooklyn for six months, and me and one of my brothers used to go to Prospect Park to play handball. Every day, the Italian boys would chase us home. "You niggers better get outta here!" *Every* day. I said, "Look at this, I used to chase, now *I'm* being chased."

By 1998, I had been drinking and drugging for forty years. I was very promiscuous, did anything to get the next high. Everybody in my building I harassed. I knocked on doors for a drink. I begged for money. The manager called me the nuisance of the building. I got clean so he wouldn't kick me out. When I got clean, I started thinking about the life I used to live, so I got tested for HIV. It was negative.

I was six months clean when I met him: Boo. We were in a recovery program together. I was thinking of what I'd like to do with my life, and that I'd like to meet somebody, and here comes this young cat. He was ten years younger than me. He had a nice smile, he brought me flowers, he'd take me bowling. I had been doing so many negative things that this was a good change.

The virus can lay dormant for years, so after I saw Boo for a while something told me to go get tested again. This time, I tested positive. I was so upset. I asked the counselor at our recovery program to sit with me when I told Boo I had the virus. Boo was so angry at me. He started yelling, "Oh, man! You did this to *me*? My life is *over*." I apologized to him over and over. "I'm sorry, Boo. I'm so sorry. You should get tested. Please get tested."

Boo stopped coming around. And then he wrote me a letter. He said, "Linda, can you forgive me? I know I acted real stupid the way I screamed and yelled at you. I'm sorry. I shouldn't have acted that way because I had the virus already. I've had it for six years." I said to myself, *Damn! Maybe he gave it to me.*

Boo still sends me cards. Says he'll always love me. That ain't love.

When Adam graduated from Colgate University,

the old man put him on a ship and sent him

to Europe and Egypt for three months. He wanted to make

Adam forget me. But there was no forgetting *me*.

ISABEL POWELL

# Isabel Powell, 93

FIRST WIFE OF ADAM CLAYTON POWELL JR.

I was about twenty-two when I met Adam. He was just as handsome as he could be. He was a preacher's son and I was a dancer at the Cotton Club. His father, Adam Clayton Powell Sr., was pastor of Abyssinian Baptist Church. Mother Powell was always sweet to me, but the old man wanted me to disappear because I was a stage girl. He liked me, but he didn't like me for Adam because he wanted Adam to take over the church. He took Adam before the deacon board, as a matter of fact. And Adam stood up and told them, "If I can't have Bunny Girl, I don't want the church." I met him at Easter time, so he called me Bunny Girl and I called him Bunny Boy.

I was a soubrette at the Cotton Club, one who leads the chorus line. Then, I was in three Broadway shows. *Harlem* was the first show. Then *Bomboola*. And the third one . . . that third one escapes me all the time. My sister, Fredi Washington, was in *Imitation of Life*, the original movie made in the thirties. She played the black woman who tries to pass for white.

When Adam graduated from Colgate University, the old man put him on a ship and sent him to Europe and Egypt for three months. He wanted to make Adam forget me. But there was no forgetting *me*. Adam brought me back twelve valves of the most exquisite flower oil. Pure oil. I gave most of it away but I kept one valve and had a great, big bottle of perfume made from it. I still have a little bit left in that bottle.

Adam really cared about the people of Harlem. He fought against high rents in those run-down tenements. When Con Edison wouldn't hire blacks, he got people to go to their office and pay their utility bills with coins. Adam was a great organizer.

There was a Jewish diamond merchant on the corner of 125th and Seventh, right where the state office building named for Adam stands today. The owner liked Adam. He told Adam, he said, "You can either have a donation of a thousand dollars or this diamond ring." The man said he smuggled the diamond out of Nazi Germany in his rectum. It was five carats. Adam took the ring and gave it to me when he proposed, this very ring I have on my finger. From the ass of a Jew to my finger.

The old man finally came around. He baptized me at Abyssinian. But when he put his hand over my face and dunked me in the baptismal pool, I thought for sure he was trying to drown me. I came up fighting. It was a sight.

Adam and I were married twelve years. I was never made so happy. But then Adam met Hazel Scott. She was a famous jazz singer and actress. I was hurt, not angry. Fredi, my sister, insisted that I leave Adam when I found out. So I went to Reno and got the divorce. I never talked to him about it. I just went. I've got a copy of the *Amsterdam News* that shows me sitting at the train station. The headline says, "Going to Reno to Divorce Best Husband in the World." I used to tell everybody that: "Adam's the best husband in the world." And he was. If I had a lick of sense, I would never have divorced him. People say to me, "But he had a woman on the side." I say, "What husband doesn't?"

The people who are invading our community now,
six years ago they wanted no part of it. But . . . they're coming
across the border: 110th Street. We should have put a fence up
like they did for Mexico, know what I mean?

JIM ELLIOTT

# Jim Elliott, 59

## OWNER OF VITAMIN STORE

Twelve years ago, Harlem had only one vitamin store so I decided to open one. I'd say that seventy percent of my customers are senior citizens, and they are funny. They . . . are . . . *funny*. One lady came in, a redbone, she was in her sixties and a little overweight. Hair was well groomed but her lipstick went outside the lines a little bit. She said, "What you got in here to make men healthy?" She said her man had too many knots in his pants. I said, "If a man can't urinate, he should see a doctor." She said, "I said he had *nots* in pants. Not long enough, not hard enough, not often enough."

I was explaining to one customer that many black people have problems with blood pressure. She said, "I ain't black. I'm American Indian." I said, "Oh, what tribe?" She said, "Nap-a-ho." One lady, she came in. She was eighty-six. Had about three teeth. She wanted garlic pills for her blood pressure. She said, "And don't give me the ones that smell 'cause I'm still kicking it, baby."

The older men get embarrassed. They'll come in, "What kind of 'Afro-disiacs' you got? I really don't need them, I just want to know." I had one older guy walk out of here with fifty dollars' worth of stuff and he said, "It ain't for me."

You might think I was a psychologist. Customers come bearing *everything*. I keep four or five chairs in the back because people like to sit down and talk. They'll talk about family problems, and being put out of their apartment, and somebody's kid quit school. Doesn't have anything to do with vitamins, but I talk with them.

Harlem was rough back when I opened the store. Drug dealers on the corner, people robbed at gunpoint, you name it. We had to close the doors at five o'clock. The people who are invading our community now, six years ago they wanted no part of it. But because of the escalating rents downtown, and the drop in crime, they're coming across the border: 110th Street. We should have put a fence up like they did for Mexico, know what I mean?

Now that things are looking brighter, they're pushing out small businesses. A hotel is going up to my left and another one to my right. A shopping center is in the works. Six years ago, there were approximately twenty-five black-owned businesses on 125th. Today, there are less than ten. All we want is the same tax breaks and loans big corporations get for investing in this community.

When my lease expires in 2002, my rent is going to increase from eighteen hundred dollars a month to *eight thousand dollars* a month. I told my landlord, "I've been a good tenant. I pay my rent on time. I take care of your building." But it didn't matter. Either I have to pay or I have to go. And where do we go? Not the Bronx. The Koreans say, "You can't come up here. This is ours." Not to Washington Heights. The Dominicans say, "You can't come up here. This is ours." So we're losing our heritage. Got Chinese people opening up restaurants called Big Mama's Soul Food.

I believe that if you take care of your body as well as you take care of your automobile, you'll have long life. That's why I named my business Long Life Vitamins. But if I had enough foresight, I would have given it another name. Maybe: Short Lived. Eighteen West 125th Street. That's my address. But don't be surprised if I'm not here when you look me up.

*[Author's update: Long Life Vitamins moved in April 2002.]*

When I told some of my friends I wanted

to move to Harlem, they said, "You're crazy!"

TONY MORGAN

# Tony Morgan, 36

GRAPHIC DESIGNER

For twelve years, I ran my business from my apartment on West Houston Street in Greenwich Village. I do graphic design. Have a small number of gallery clients in SoHo. In 1998, I was thinking of moving my business to Harlem, but I was a little concerned what my clients would think. But they thought it was a fantastic idea. One was even looking for space in Harlem to open a gallery. But when I told some of my friends I wanted to move to Harlem, they said, "You're crazy!" They were concerned about the crime rate.

Like most white people south of 96th Street, I had not ventured up to Harlem much. A black friend of mine, who lives on 118th Street, said a home in Harlem would be a great investment. He said, "Get in while you can; in two or three years they're not going to be affordable anymore." He was right.

At one point there was a glut of properties that were burned out, boarded up, abandoned—shells. They couldn't give them away. But, suddenly, they were getting snapped up. Everybody knew somebody who was looking up here. You had people like me who bought to live or work out of the buildings. And you had speculators who grabbed properties and immediately flipped them for sizable profit.

When I first started looking, shells in Harlem were going for eighty thousand dollars. It took six months to sell my apartment in the Village, and in that six months those same shells were going for two hundred thousand dollars—boarded-up shells with no detailing. If I would have waited another six months, I wouldn't have been able to afford it.

My house is four stories plus a cellar. Structurally, it's quite solid: generous rooms, great detailing, tall ceilings. You walk in here and you see a gorgeous place, but I didn't walk in and find it this way. Windows were smashed. Leaves were all over the floors. It looked like a war zone. It needed a new roof, new plumbing, new electric. All the woodwork in the house was painted: The dining room was orange, a fireplace was pink and brown. Ironically, the paint, awful as it was, preserved the wood. It took a lot of renovating, but today the house might sell for a million dollars. And if the area continues to improve—and I think it will—it might be worth double that in two years.

A lot of longtime residents can no longer afford housing in Harlem and have to move elsewhere. That's unfortunate, but that's economics. If they do get pushed out and have to move to, say, the Bronx, then somebody is getting pushed out of the Bronx to make room for them. I got pushed out of downtown.

Harlem has a glorious African-American history. But there was a glorious history before that. My house was built around 1880. It's part of a row of houses built at the same time. The original European inhabitants were Dutch immigrants. Later, Harlem was the suburbs to European immigrants who worked in downtown Manhattan. During that time, some of the most opulent churches, theaters, and apartments in the city were built in Harlem.

I remember the good ol' days of Greenwich Village, during the early 1990s. I remember SoHo, when it was new and fresh and mostly galleries, not all the expensive boutiques there now. It used to be a very beautiful place, but it's not like that anymore. Manhattan changes. Harlem changes. America changes. Everything changes.

Harlem is huge. There's room for everybody.

*[Author's update: Tony Morgan sold his brownstone and moved to upstate New York in March 2002.]*

There's no other community in New York

where you see as many book vendors per square foot

as you do on 125th Street.

They could be selling anything—candles, incense—but they're

selling books. And this is because they recognize

what Louis Michaux always recognized, that folks in Harlem

love to read.

MARIE BROWN

# Marie Brown, *61*

LITERARY AGENT

There's a lot I miss about the Harlem of the fifties and sixties. I miss Frank's, which was this fabulous, white-tablecloth restaurant, with waiters in tuxedoes. My mother's first cousin, Ralph, took me there when I was a teenager visiting from Philadelphia. Ralph knew everybody at Frank's because he was the pharmacist at the Hotel Theresa. Ralph also took me to Club Baby Grand and Sugar Ray's, where I sipped Shirley Temples like I was grown. I miss those places, too. But what I miss most is Louis Michaux's bookstore.

In 1967, Philadelphia just got to be too small, so my best friend and I moved to New York. That's when I started to spend a lot of time uptown. And that's when I discovered Mr. Michaux's bookstore. It was a place where not only people like Malcom X and other great thinkers visited, but ordinary people. I've always had this great love of books, and an affinity for book people, so I loved that place. There were no other bookstores of any renown in the city that focused on black culture and history, so this was the destination.

Michaux's was at the site of what's now Adam Clayton Powell State Office building. There was this whole strip of stores there, little community shops—Tree of Life health food store and places like that. The bookstore was a typical Harlem storefront, except that the exterior was blanketed with large, hand-painted signs and posters: "The House of Common Sense," "Home of Proper Propaganda." The signs let you know that this was no ordinary bookstore. It was a house of knowledge for black people.

When you walked in, it was small and crowded. It was dimly lit and smelled like old books. The bookcases were along the walls and jammed with vast volumes. Posters of black legends were all around: Booker T. Washington, Frederick Douglass, Harriet Tubman. But the real emphasis was what was on the shelves, not on decor.

Louis Michaux was always there, sitting in a chair, having exchanges with customers. He was not as much holding court as he was just participating in conversations about black life—culture, history, politics. He seemed to know everything. It was as if he had read and memorized every book in his store. He was an older man. Small, quiet. But powerful. Not the type who raised his voice and waved his arms to expound. You felt you were in the presence of a scholar. But he was kind, approachable, never aloof. I always felt that Louis Michaux didn't just want you to buy a book, he wanted you to know something, to learn something. Yes, he operated as a retail business, but you felt he was doing what he could to preserve the knowledge of who his people really are, and how important they are in world history.

We have the Liberation Bookstore now, we have Hue-Man, we have the bookshops in the Studio Museum and the Schomburg. But when you witness all those booksellers on the sidewalks of 125th Street, you are witnessing Mr. Michaux's true legacy. There's no other community in New York where you see as many book vendors per square foot as you do on 125th Street. They could be selling anything—candles, incense—but they're selling books. And this is because they recognize what Louis Michaux always recognized, that folks in Harlem love to read.

Louis Michaux wasn't just a bookseller. He was a purveyor of knowledge, a man who had a great love of his people. Just being in Michaux's gave you a sense of empowerment. I miss that place.

"A spa in Harlem? You really want to open a spa

in Harlem?" That's what everybody asked my husband and me.

A lot of people flat out said, "It ain't gonna work."

DR. CYNTHIA GRACE

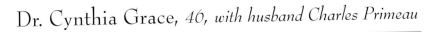

# Dr. Cynthia Grace, *46, with husband Charles Primeau*

SPA OWNERS

"A spa in Harlem? You really want to open a spa in Harlem?" That's what everybody asked my husband and me. A lot of people flat out said, "It ain't gonna work." I guess to many people it's an oxymoron. But you wouldn't think that if you really knew Harlem.

I grew up in upstate New York, but I moved to Harlem in the 1970s. There's diversity here in every way: racially, economically, you name it. Right on this street you have a beauty salon, a judge, people on welfare, a church. And some of the ladies on the block, quite frankly, dress in a manner that makes you wonder about the nature of their profession.

Soon after we opened the spa, this tall black lady strutted in wearing cheetah-print pants. She was beautiful, but you could tell that the streets had worn her down. She looked about forty, but she was probably younger. She had on dark shades, bright lipstick, and a full, curly wig. A real character. She came to the reception desk and said to my husband, "Do you do waxing here?" My husband said, "Yes, we do." She said, "Good, 'cause I want the crack of my ass waxed. Take *all* that hair out." My husband said, "Well, I think we can do that." I think she was testing us, letting us know she's in the neighborhood, but there's actually a name for that service: a Brazilian bikini wax.

Typically, people associate spas with affluence, and we get those people. I'll get into trouble if I name names, but we've had probably the country's best-known black attorney and one of Hollywood's most talented black male actors—with an Oscar. [*Laughs.*] But we've also had people who've never had a facial or massage in their life.

One time, three siblings came in. You could tell they weren't well off. One of the sisters said, "Our mother has worked so hard all her life. She never does anything for herself. So we want to treat her to your spa. It's a surprise."

Later, one of the daughters brought the mother, who was about sixty. She looked like she had had a hard life. The mother looked around and said, "Oh, no. I can't deal with this." I said, "What can we do to make you feel more comfortable?" The massage therapist even came out to explain the treatment.

The mother finally went into the room, but I didn't think she would stay. You know how some older folks are about taking off their clothes. But half an hour passed and she hadn't come out. Forty-five minutes. An hour later she came out wearing a robe, smiling, and waving her arms in the air. She went into the aesthetician's room for her facial. I said, "Okay, you go, girl!"

I checked on her during the facial. She said, "You know, I hate to put those dirty clothes back on." I said, "I hate to spoil the surprise, but your children are on their way. They've bought you a new outfit." She started to tear, I started to tear, the aesthetician started to tear.

Her children brought her a purple African robe and a gold and purple turban. She put the outfit on and looked six inches taller. When she was leaving I said, "You look so *beautiful.*" She said, in an aristocratic tone, "I'll be back."

Thousands of tourists come to Harlem churches

to hear gospel. . . . They want to know how it is that you

may not have food on your table or money in your pocket

and sound so happy.

JAMES FORD

# James Ford, 55

CHURCH DEACON

Thousands of tourists come to Harlem churches to hear gospel. I call this reverse missionary work: Instead of us going out to foreign lands, they come to us. They want to know how it is that you may not have food on your table or money in your pocket and sound so happy.

The tourists are very apprehensive at first, pretty stiff. So first thing we do is try to loosen them up. I say, "We're going to begin with a little gospel exercise. Come on, put your hands together like this." [*Clap. Clap. Clap. Clap.*] They begin to smile. Then I say, "Take your coat off. We're all friends here." They pull their coats off. Then we pass out tambourines so they can be part of the music. Then I say, "Let's sing that old spiritual 'Amen.'" I use that one because it's a one-word song: A-men. A-men. A-men, a-men, a-men. No matter what language you speak, you can handle "Amen." By the end of the service, they're on their feet singing. A man from Germany told me: "You should franchise dis church overseas. If ve had church like dis at home, ve go more often."

I know how he feels. When I first joined Memorial Baptist ten years ago, I really wanted to be part of the music. A couple of years ago, the drummer for our Wednesday service didn't show up. The pastor said, "Somebody got to play some drums here."

I'm really just a frustrated musician. If I had my way, I would have been in show business long time ago. So I volunteered to play the drums. But I didn't know how. I kept the beat, but I couldn't keep the *right* beat. See, on a four-four count, black people clap on two and four. Europeans clap on one and three. So I was playing on one and three. The pastor said, "Forget the drums."

One day, when hardly anybody was around, I humbled myself and asked Robert Livingston to teach me how to play. Robert's a member of the church. At the time, he was eight years old. Robert's big brother plays drums at the regular Sunday service and he taught Robert how to play. Robert asked me, "Are you sure?"

First thing Robert did was show me how to hold the sticks. I was holding them all wrong. Then he taught me patience. Put someone behind a set a drums for the first time and they usually go crazy, banging everything as hard and fast as you can. That's what I was doing. Robert said, "No, no, no. Just the bass." BOOM. BOOM. BOOM. BOOM. "Good. Stay with that." After a while he showed me how to bring in the snare. BOOM-DAT.-BOOM-DAT.BOOM-DAT.BOOM-DAT. It started getting good to me. I said, "What's next?" He said, "Just keep practicing that."

I practiced every day because I knew that, one Sunday, Robert's big brother wouldn't show up. I *hoped* he wouldn't show up. It's like being an understudy in a Broadway play. You don't wish bad on anyone, but somebody's got to get sick for you to perform.

Sure enough, one Sunday, Robert's brother didn't show. My heart was like, *dat-dat-dat-dat-dat-dat-dat-dat*. I looked over at my mother. She gave me a look like, *Don't you embarrass me, boy!* I started playing. Quietly. *Boom-dat. Boom-dat.* Real low. Just enough to let them know I was there. *Boom-dat.* But not really making much noise. *Boom-dat.* After the service, I asked Robert how I did. There I was a grown man uptight about the opinion of an eight-year-old. He thought about it and said, "You did all right."

I felt so good.

I hear feelings when black people sing.

When I hear gospel in Harlem, I feel more open to God.

YUKO ICHIOKA

# Yuko Ichioka, 36

GOSPEL SINGER

The first time I heard gospel music in Japan was in the movie *Sister Act* with Whoopi Goldberg. She was dancing and singing and clapping and the choir was following her. I was amazed. So when I came to New York four years ago, one of the first things I did was take a gospel bus tour of Harlem.

When I walked into the St. Stephen A. M. E. Church, the ushers were all dressed in white and the choir was in pretty robes. I had never seen that. Everything was call and response: The pastor said something and everybody said, "Aaa-men." Then the drums started beating, and the organ started playing, and the choir started singing, and everybody was shaking tambourines.

I saw some women getting the Holy Ghost; they were going higher and higher with their emotions and dancing in a trance. The people were so happy. They were singing about love, and hope, and joy. That was really touching to my heart. I said, *I want to sing like that.*

When I first started going to church in Harlem, some people looked at me mean. They didn't know why I was there. But after I went to church for a while, I began to melt this ice.

I would take the number 2 or 3 train to 116th street and walk a block to the church. A lot of guys teased me. They said, "Hey, China doll. What's up, Chinese girl?" My friends asked me, "Aren't you scared to walk from the subway station to the church?" I said, "No, I just smile and sing gospel music when I walk and nobody bothers me." I sing songs like:

*Victory is mine,*
*Victory is mine,*
*Victory today is mine.*
*I told Satan to get thee behind.*
*Victory today is mine.*

When you sing gospel, you have to show your feelings. But Japanese have a different cultural background. We keep our feelings inside. Japanese people only show their emotions at a funeral, like my grandmother's funeral.

I'm from Amagasaki city. It's a merchant town near Osaka. When I was five years old, my grandmother died. Everybody got together and cried. In Japan, we don't bury people. We cremate. I didn't really know what death was, but I knew it turned you into ashes.

Seven days after my grandmother died, my cousin, Eiji, was killed in a car accident. We were the same age. We grew up together like a brother and sister. I was so scared: Eiji was going to turn into ashes.

At the funeral, everybody was crying, crying, crying. My auntie said, "Oh, your grandmother loved Eiji so much. She took him because he was her favorite." Even at five, I was a little sarcastic maybe. Because I was thinking, *Thank God I wasn't her favorite.*

Gospel is really popular in Japan right now. I think people want to feel happy and warm, and they can feel that through this music. I'm studying music and I learned that during slavery, black people could only experience freedom through music in church. I hear feelings when black people sing. When I hear gospel in Harlem, I feel more open to God.

*[Author's update: In April 2003, Yuko Ichioka moved back to Japan, where she teaches gospel.]*

When I came up from the subway, I said, "Oh, man, I'm lost!" But then I saw the Apollo and it blew me away. I said, *Wow, this is it! I'm in Harlem!* I had never been to Harlem before, but I just knew I belonged here.

BRYAN COLLIER

# Bryan Collier, *34*

AUTHOR AND ARTIST

I was lost, that's how I ended up in Harlem for the first time. I was a student at the Pratt Institute downtown. It was 1985, my freshman year. I had a class project to see an expressionistic exhibition at the Met, the Metropolitan Museum of Art, then write a paper. That was going to be my first experience on the subway. I'm from Pocomoke City in Maryland, Lower Eastern Shore. I had never been on the subway before so, of course, I didn't understand the train lines.

I called myself taking the number 6 to 86th Street, but somehow I ended up taking the A train all the way up to 125th. Don't ask. When I came up from the subway, I said, "Oh, man, I'm lost!" But then I saw the Apollo and it blew me away. I said, *Wow, this is it! I'm in Harlem!* I had never been to Harlem before, but I just knew I belonged here. It felt near to me. It was like something came up out of the street and hugged me.

It was a Saturday morning. Eleven-ish. People were out, but it wasn't crowded. I sort of walked around in a daze. I'm drawn to architecture so my eyes were drawn to that first. The brownstones looked like chocolate. I saw ragged awnings over windows, dirty awnings, but I imagined how they once looked, all bright and colorful. Buildings all dressed up. I looked at the curves of the carvings along the rooftops and the way the shadows fell on the stoops, sort of like folded paper. Colors, shadows, lines—that's what spoke to me first.

Then I heard pieces of conversations on the street that formed this sort of symphony. People talking to each other, not to me. But it was *for* me because I was meant to be there.

That was back in the day when they had African vendors who set up tables all up and down 125th. They sold everything: socks, toothpaste, batteries. You had this guy's music competing with that guy's music. It was a good vibe. But the store owners hated it because you didn't need them. You could get anything you needed on the street. 125th Street was jumping.

It was my first time in Harlem, but the ordinary movement of people was warm and familiar. It's how black people everywhere move. There was a beat and a rhythm that I knew. And if an old lady walked by, I knew what was in her purse because I know what my grandmother carried in her purse: peppermints, a pair of white gloves, a little package of tissue, and a lot of loose change.

I hope I wasn't looking like a tourist, but I was checking out stuff all around me. It's like when you meet somebody for the first time and you know you used to know them. You just connect. Harlem was like that. We didn't know each other but we *did* know each other.

Before I knew it, I had walked all the way to the edge of Central Park, on 110th. I was buzzing with all these feelings and thoughts so I kept going. I ended up walking all the way to the Met.

I love to visit places,

but I would never leave Harlem.

Last year I went to St. Martin. Year before that I went to

Grenada. But I always want to get back to Harlem.

And The Corner.

GREGORY CIVERS

# Gregory Civers, *15*

STUDENT

I learned to play chess when I was five. I'm very curious. If I see something new, I like to figure it out. I think that's why I was interested in chess. I'd see these grown men on the corner of 135th and Fifth, moving little objects on a board, and wanted to know what they were doing. That's how I became the first kid to play chess on The Corner.

I live in the Lincoln projects. I grew up here. But I'm not like a lot of the other kids. They like to be destructive. I like to be creative. So this man named Sonny said I should become a chess player to develop my mind. Sonny introduced chess to the projects. He brings sets out here almost every day so people can play.

They play serious chess on The Corner, but the players accepted me with open arms. I think they were surprised a kid wanted to learn, so they taught me. Mr. Gaylord taught me the most. He started with correcting the names of the pieces. He said, "Son, this is a 'knight,' not a 'horsey.'" Sometimes, I still accidentally call a knight a horsey. You should see the looks I get. Things you learn when you're young, they stick with you.

People find it strange that I'm always out here. My friends say, "Aw, why you want to play chess?" Well, I do do other things. But I'd rather play chess. I'll say to my parents, "I'm going to The Corner." I'm usually the first one out here so I help Sonny unpack the van. Then I'll play Sonny one or two games. I'm a strong player, so Sonny doesn't take his game down. No one takes their game down. It wouldn't be a challenge if people took their game down. We play to push each other. Then I go back home and mingle with friends. If nothing's going on, like playing basketball or skating, I'll come back to The Corner. Sometimes I'll stay until Sonny packs up, which is usually about eight o'clock.

It's a very noisy intersection, 135th and Fifth. You have cars going back and forth across the bridge to the Bronx. You have the highway going downtown. You have buses. There are a lot of stores around here so you have delivery trucks. But I don't hear the world when I play chess. A fire engine could go by, but all my focus is on the game. I can't even hear my mother call me to do the dishes.

The advanced players sit over in the shade. They bring their own sets. Sometimes they play until two, three, four in the morning. They *really* love the game. If I want a game after Sonny leaves, I'll play with them. My parents sit on the bench and watch. My parents are happy that I love chess. You can get into a fight on the basketball court, but no one's going to throw fists over a chessboard.

They're very generous on The Corner. A lot of the advanced players will take time to help you. One time, a guy beat me and then he broke down the last ten or fifteen moves and showed me other options.

I always apply chess to life. There are things that I might think I'm not able to do, but I'll still try. I'm not afraid to mess up. Even if you mess up, you'll learn something. Chess taught me that.

I love to visit places, but I would never leave Harlem. Last year I went to St. Martin. Year before that I went to Grenada. But I always want to get back to Harlem. And The Corner.

I moved to Harlem in 1944, near the end of the war.

I was in my twenties. If I had the money, I would

have gone right . . . back . . . home.

RUTH LEVELL

# Ruth Levell, 81

YMCA VOLUNTEER

I grew up in Jamaica. A rural town called St. Elizabeth. St. Elizabeth was *beautiful*. The earth was red. The beaches were so blue. The air smelled green, like vegetation.

Marcus Garvey was a friend of my neighbors. Marcus Garvey was from Jamaica but he made a name for himself in Harlem. He founded the UNIA (Universal Negro Improvement Association) and he promoted self-reliance among black people. He also started a shipping company called the Black Star Line, which was supposed to take black people back to Africa.

Marcus Garvey came to visit my neighbors in St. Elizabeth when I was seven or eight. I remember thinking that he was small for a man. But I knew he was important because he was wearing a uniform and this admiral-looking hat, somewhat like the hat our governor wore. He sat me on his knee and he was bouncing me up and down. But I hadn't a clue who he was.

I moved to Harlem in 1944, near the end of the war. I was in my twenties. If I had the money, I would have gone right . . . back . . . *home*. When you live in Jamaica, you grow up thinking the streets in New York are paved with gold. Tourists would come to Jamaica and spend so much money. We heard about Coney Island and the World's Fair. And to come here and see conditions that were contrary to the myth, that was a bit surprising.

I heard that there was a five-and-dime on 116th Street, so I walked up there. I wanted to see with my own eyes a store that sold everything for five and ten cents. But I found that it wasn't really so. Some things cost more, you know. I asked the clerks about it, but I couldn't really understand what they were saying. Their accent was so different. I suppose they couldn't understand my accent, either: "Cho! Wha' dis? De sign say five . . . an' . . . dime."

When I came, all the young men were away at war so it was easy to find housing. I was living on 110th Street, in an apartment near Central Park. The whole building was filled with Jamaicans. In those days, people from the Caribbean were very clannish. People from Barbados stayed with their own; people from Trinidad stayed together.

Shortly after I got here, a relative took me to the YMCA for tea. They had a nice little restaurant there. You might bump into Langston Hughes or Ethel Waters or Billy Eckstine. Oh, that Billy Eckstine! He had that *voice* and he was so good looking, like a black Clark Gable. My boyfriend took me to Club Ebony to hear Billy Eckstine. As he was singing, Billy Eckstine came to our table and serenaded me. My boyfriend said, "We're not coming back to this club anymore."

You'd see all the black men in uniform at the Y—the soldiers and sailors who weren't welcome in hotels downtown. They also had a theater in the Y. The Y was also a kind of trade school. They taught people to sew, or secretarial skills. The Y was the hub for black people. It was *the* place to go.

One saturday afternoon in 1958, my mother and I went to Blumstein's department store on 125th Street. Blumstein's was like a small Macy's. It's been closed forever, but the sign is still on the building. When we came into the store, we noticed that Martin Luther King Jr. was there to promote his book, *Stride Toward Freedom*. I stood in line and got a book, and he signed it. I spoke to him. He was very pleasant, very dignified. My mother and I went to look at linens; then we heard a woman scream and a big commotion.

Someone shouted that Dr. King had been stabbed.

I was just going off duty at Harlem Hospital when they brought Dr. Martin Luther King into the emergency room on a stretcher. He was conscious and a letter opener was protruding from his chest. The letter opener shook every time his heart beat.

CHARLES FELTON

# Charles Felton, M.D., 75

ASSOCIATE DIRECTOR OF MEDICINE
AT HARLEM HOSPITAL

I was just going off duty at Harlem Hospital when they brought Dr. Martin Luther King into the emergency room on a stretcher. He was conscious and a letter opener was protruding from his chest. The letter opener shook every time his heart beat.

It was a Saturday afternoon in September of 1958. I was an intern and I was supposed to get off at twelve, but in the emergency room you never get off on time. My wife, who was also an intern at the hospital, was sitting in a car just outside the emergency room entrance, waiting for me. Half a minute later and I would have been gone.

There was no active bleeding from Dr. King's wound, but I wanted to know if that blade was affecting his heart. If blood was flooding his chest, he could have died at any moment. We stripped him to the waist. He was a very well-built man, solid. I said, "I'm going to examine your chest now, Dr. King." I listened to his chest and his lungs. I started getting an EKG on him. He was very calm. If he was praying, he was praying to himself.

King had been down at a store on 125th Street, autographing a book he wrote. A woman, a black woman who was crazed, stabbed him in the chest as he sat there. His aides did the right thing by not removing the blade. It would have made matters worse. Nobody knew exactly how deep the blade went until they opened him up in surgery, but it was resting right up against the aorta, the biggest artery. The aorta's width is a little larger than a nickel. There's a lot of pressure in it. That's why the blade moved every time his heart beat. If he had sneezed, it could have killed him.

Word that Dr. King was in the emergency room spread around the hospital in a matter of minutes. What's interesting is that one of my fellow interns at the hospital was Bob Wilson. Bob and Martin Luther King had been roommates at Boston University. Bob was in pre-med and Dr. King was studying theology. Bob Wilson came in and said, "Hello, Martin. How are you doing?" Dr. King said, "I've been better."

Right about that time, here comes the surgical team, saying, "Get out of the way! Get out of the way!" They took Dr. King to surgery and waited for Dr. Maynard to arrive. Dr. Aubré Maynard was head of surgery. He was a West Indian fellow, a fine surgeon. When Dr. King arrived at the hospital, Dr. Maynard was way downtown in a movie theater. They put out a call for him. As long as Dr. King was stable and not in any distress, they had time to wait for Dr. Maynard, who performed the operation which led to Dr. King's full recovery.

Dr. King was in the hospital for about two or three weeks. Bob Wilson and I would go visit him in the evenings. We'd sit and talk about some of the work he was doing and the two of them would talk about school. I met Dr. King's wife, Coretta, who was there every day.

A year later, I flew down to Montgomery, Alabama, for basic training at Maxwell Air Force base. I went over to Dr. King's church. He was away, but Coretta invited me in for coffee. I never got to see Dr. King again before he was killed ten years later.

Often, teachers announce, "Okay, kids, we have ten or twenty minutes before we have to go," and I just want to shoot them. Children should spend a *whole* day here. There's so much to learn.

WILHELMINA ROBERTS WYNN

# Wilhelmina Roberts Wynn, *87*

TOUR GUIDE AT SCHOMBURG CENTER
FOR RESEARCH IN BLACK CULTURE

I've worked at the Schomburg for, well . . . a lot of years. The Schomburg is a library, a museum, and a performing arts center all rolled into one. I am a docent, a trained tour guide. I especially enjoy giving tours to schoolchildren. They like when the tour stops at the cosmogram, which is on the floor of the atrium. The cosmogram is a work of art by Houston Conwill, and it's based on a poem by Langston Hughes, "The Negro Speaks of Rivers." The verses of the poem appear throughout the cosmogram and the rivers mentioned in the poem run through it: the Euphrates, the Congo, the Nile, and the Mississippi. The cosmogram also contains the birth dates of Langston Hughes and Arthur Schomburg, who was a black Puerto Rican.

I always tell the children the story about Arthur Schomburg. I say, "When he was in school he asked his teacher to tell him something about the history of black people. The legend goes that the teacher said, 'You have no heroes. You have no great moments.' " Now, at that point, I ask the children, "How do you think he felt when his teacher said that?" Someone will say, "He felt bad." I say, "Who else?" I keep asking until I get the right answer: "He was *mad*." I say, "Good. *Very* good. He was so mad that he went out and collected everything he could about blacks and their history. He collected books, artifacts, photographs, anything that demonstrated that blacks *did* have heroes and great moments in history. Then, when he came to New York at eighteen, he lived in Brooklyn and continued to collect. He had so many books and photographs and artifacts that he had to either move out of his home or give it all away. Well, children, someone heard about his collection and wanted him to sell it to the New York Public Library, which he did. Eventually, the collection was moved here."

Then, I pick one of the students and say, "Why don't you read Langston Hughes's poem aloud for us?" They always have trouble when they get to the line, "I heard the singing of the Mississippi when Abe Lincoln went down to New Orleans, and I've seen its muddy bosom turn all golden in the sunset." Well, the children always mispronounce "bosom." I say, "It's not bahsum. It's boozem." Then I say, "What's a 'bosom'?" One bright child might say, "It's the upper part of a woman's anatomy." Everyone giggles. One time, a girl said, "The bosom is near your heart." I said, "That is right. I *like* that." I say, "It's where a mother holds her baby, her bosom."

At the end of my comments, I ask one child to come and stand in the middle of the cosmogram. I say, "What do you see?" The child says, "I see a fish." I say, "That's true. But what else?" The child says, "I see some words, 'My soul has grown deep like the rivers.' " I say, "That's right. But there's something you can't see. Right under the fish and those words, there's a small, stainless steel box, and in that box are some of Langston Hughes's remains, his ashes." They're amazed. I say, "There are five other boxes with his remains, and they were sent to places around the world. But one of them is right under your feet." They say, "Wow!"

Often, teachers announce, "Okay, kids, we have ten or twenty minutes before we have to go," and I just want to shoot them. Children should spend a *whole* day here. There's so much to learn.

I *am* Harlem! When people around the world

think of Harlem, they think of the food at Sylvia's:

my fried chicken, my collards, my corn bread. I've fed Robert F.

Kennedy, Muhammad Ali, Madonna, Malcolm X.

SYLVIA WOODS

# Sylvia Woods, 76

## RESTAURANT OWNER

I *am* Harlem! When people around the world think of Harlem, they think of the food at Sylvia's: my fried chicken, my collards, my corn bread. I've fed Robert F. Kennedy, Muhammad Ali, Madonna, Malcolm X. And I did it all with Herbert by my side.

In 1937, I met Herbert Woods in a bean patch in Hemingway, South Carolina. I was eleven and Herbert was twelve. We were picking green peas, and had our eyes on each other all day long. Herbert was a pretty, brown color and he had such kind eyes. He was barefoot and his knees poked out of his raggedy overalls, but we didn't call them overalls back then. We called them "overhauls" because they were so patched up. I said to my girlfriend, "Who that little pretty boy there? I'm gonna *marry* him."

I started writing little letters to Herbert, things like: "Sugar's sweet / watermelon's red / I'll love you / 'til the day I'm dead." One time, Herbert's mother read one of my letters. She told Herbert, "You tell that little girl you don't love *nobody*. You going to college."

Herbert and I lived on opposite ends of a dirt road, so he couldn't carry my books home after school. We'd walk backward and wave frantically to each other. He'd smile and say, "Bye." I'd smile and say, "Bye." We'd walk backward a bit more and he'd say, "Bye." I'd say, "Bye." We'd walk some more and he'd say, "Bye." I'd say, "Bye." One time, I tripped and fell in a puddle. Herbert pretended like he didn't see.

My mother let me start taking company when I was fourteen, but only on a Wednesday, which was a half day in the field, and on a Sunday. Herbert and I would sit alone in the living room, but my mother kept walking through. Herbert had to give me quick little kisses. Courting hours were six to nine. At nine o'clock, my mother would start clearing her throat. "Ugh, ugh, ughmmm."

When I was sixteen, my mom sent me to New York to learn how to be a beautician. That's how they separated me and Herbert. But Herbert had a plan. He put his age up a year and joined the Navy. See, he thought they'd send him to the Brooklyn Navy Yard, and we'd be together again. But they sent him to San Francisco. We stayed together, though, and on January 18, 1944, while Herbert was still in the Navy, we got married. We kissed so long that the minister had to break us up.

Not long after we settled in Harlem, Herbert got a job driving a taxi, and I applied for a job as a waitress at Johnson's Luncheonette on Lenox and 126th Street. I told Mr. Johnson that I had worked in a restaurant back home. But he knew I was lying. Mr. Johnson was a black man from Charleston, South Carolina, and he knew that Hemingway had just one restaurant, and it was segregated. He gave me a job anyway. I worked there for eight years, saving and saving, before Mr. Johnson approached me one day. He said, "Sylvia, how'd you like to buy the restaurant from me?" That was 1962, and that was the beginning of Sylvia's.

Herbert and I had four children. Things got so busy at the restaurant that he came to work by my side. We were inseparable from that day we met in the bean patch. And we were blessed with fifty-seven years of marriage before I lost him. It's probably best that he went first. I don't know how he would have lived without me. He loved me so.

Some call me

"The Picasso of Harlem."

But I prefer "Franco the Great."

FRANCO GASKIN

# Franco Gaskin, *73*

ARTIST

I am a painter. Some call me "The Picasso of Harlem." But I prefer "Franco the Great." My love for painting goes back to what happened to me in Panama when I was a kid.

I was born in the town of Colon. My family lived in a three-story building. Our apartment was on the top floor. When I was about two, my grandmother turned her attention for a moment. I climbed on a chair, I crawled across a table, and I fell out of a window. I landed on my head. They say my head was black and blue and big as a melon. The doctors couldn't believe I fell from that height. I was in a coma, could not speak for months.

When I got better, grown-ups would say, "That boy is *born* to live, born to live." But kids were mean to me because I had developed a speech impediment. They called me Dummy. "Run, run. Here comes Dummy." That made me withdraw into myself. I didn't talk to other kids. I didn't play with other kids. Drawing became my outlet. I taught myself to paint when I got older. By the time I was in my twenties, I was a very popular artist.

My father and grandmother moved to Harlem. They sent for me. I thought, *If I can make a good living selling my art in Panama, which is the size of a dot, I could be a millionaire in New York*. I landed in Harlem about forty-five years ago. I walked up and down 125th Street, knocking on the door of every business, asking to paint murals on their walls. They all turned me down. I did not understand because I offered to paint for free, just to make myself a name. A friend told me, "Man, no one in Harlem does anything for nothing. They think you are up to no good." So I went downtown and painted murals in Mexican restaurants. That opened the door for me to sell portraits. A few years later I tried it again uptown. I felt like a magnet was pulling me back to Harlem.

There was a riot in Harlem in 1968, when Dr. Martin Luther King was killed. There was burning and looting. Many businesses put up metal shutters, metal grates, for protection. But kids were painting graffiti on the grates. One day, John Baynes said, "Frank, I want you to paint something to cover that graffiti." He owned Theresa Fashions on 125th Street. I said, "Well, I have never painted on a grate before, but I can try."

I painted something very simple: a magnolia tree. The background was sky blue and the tree had a lot of pink blossoms. People asked me what it meant. I said, "It means I want to bloom where I was planted." I was planted in Harlem.

Over the years, I have painted hundreds of grates on 125th Street. It is the world's largest gallery. I do not see anything too spectacular about my painting, but tour buses bring the world to my feet. I have been on television in France, Germany, Brazil, Japan, and more. I could not even talk when I was a kid. But I taught myself to speak five languages and I give art lectures all over the world.

Maybe the best thing that happened to me was when the kids rejected me. It taught me. It taught me that you do not have to be what people say you are.

One time in Harlem, a lady argue with me.

She say, "Why don't you go back to your country?" I say,

"Why you hate me?" . . . I say, "I'm just trying to work

for myself because a woman

want too much that a man can't afford."

SY OUMOUKOULSHOME

# Sy Oumoukoulshome, *39*

HAIR BRAIDER

You see all those African women sitting in chairs on 125th Street? They live hard. They outside trying to get people inside the shops to braid their hair. It's cold on the street, they stopping people. It's snowing or raining on the street, they stopping people. But it's better on the street than in the shops, with forty or fifty braiders working in a room that can't fit twenty people. They working on top of each other with rats and mice and bathrooms dirty. And who own those places? Not those women. The owners say, "Oh, they live like animals in the jungle back home, so put them in a little, dirty room."

And people treat them bad on the street. People curse them, people call them names. One time, I heard a braider ask a woman, "Excuse me, miss. Braid your hair?" The woman stop and say, very angry, "You can see I got my hair done already. Do you want to braid my pubic hair?" That hurt me so bad I couldn't sleep that night, and she not even talking to me. Some people respect the braiders, give them business. But some people smack them, push them. The police give them tickets for being on the street, and that's money they cannot pay. I want to tell the women, "You don't have to take all that abuse. You have a talent. You have a skill. You have the right to make money like other people." But it's not easy for them. Some don't speak English.

I didn't speak English when I come here in 1990. I'm from West Africa. Dakar, Senegal. When I was little, my father used to pay people to come to the house and braid our hair, my sisters and me. Every six weeks, someone come to the house, someone from the same family. It's a tradition that some families in Senegal specialize in doing braids. They call them griots. It goes from generation to generation. A little kid, eight-year-old kid from a griot family can braid your hair in tiny, tiny micro braids, which is difficult to make.

Also, the griots can tell people the history of their family. Let's say you have a birthday party. The griots can come to the party and tell you from the beginning to the end who is in your family and what your family accomplish. They memorize history. When we were little, a griot would tell us about our ancestors fighting against France. In Senegal, hair braiders have respect from people. But not in Harlem.

One time in Harlem, a lady argue with me. She say, "Why don't you go back to your country?" I say, "Why you hate me?" She say, "You come here and take all our jobs and we don't have nothing." I say, "You have to get that out of your mind." I say, "When we first come to this country, we don't speak English, we don't have papers to work, we don't know nothing about America. But we survive. We just try to survive." I say, "What white people do to us, we're not supposed to do to each other. Solve the problem. I'm not the problem." I say, "I'm just trying to work for myself because a woman want too much that a man can't afford."

I'm working on getting a license to teach. I want to open a school to teach children hair braiding so when they grow up they will have a skill.

It is not a shame to braid hair.

When I first came to Abyssinian, I was about

twenty-two years old. . . . James Brown was my man. I used to

put on my bib overalls, hook up my boom box

outside the church, and dance with the kids in the middle of

the street to James Brown's music.

REV. CALVIN O. BUTTS III

# Rev. Calvin O. Butts III, *53*

### PASTOR OF ABYSSINIAN BAPTIST CHURCH

Abyssinian Baptist Church is Harlem, and Harlem is Abyssinian. The church has a long history and deep roots. It's named for an ancient country in Africa. Abyssinian was founded in Lower Manhattan in 1808. It made its way uptown, as did the African-American community, eventually moving to 138th Street here in Harlem. Our current church was erected in 1923, and almost every significant personality and every significant event in the history of Harlem has been connected to Abyssinian.

The dynamic duo of Adam Clayton Powell Sr. and Adam Clayton Powell Jr. were pastors. Adam Sr. was one of the founders of the NAACP. He was so prominent that he built the largest Protestant congregation in America, black or white. Adam Jr. was an effective activist and the first real representative of black people in the U.S. Congress.

So many artists have performed in our sanctuary: tap dancer Bill "Bojangles" Robinson, opera singers Leontyne Price and Kathleen Battle, Whitney Houston before she blew up, the entire Marsalis family—Wynton, Branford, Ellis. Great leaders have spoken here: Malcolm X, educator and activist Mary McLeod Bethune, Ethiopian Emperor Haile Selassie, Minister Louis Farrakhan.

Today, when you talk about rebuilding Harlem, Abyssinian has parlayed—from 1989 until today—$50,000 into $250 million. We have built the largest supermarket on Manhattan island here in Harlem. We're building a major commercial center at 125th Street and Malcolm X Boulevard, and the first high school erected in Harlem in fifty years.

We've built affordable housing for senior citizens and housing for middle- and upper-income people, and have not displaced—that's very important to underscore—we have not displaced any residents of this community.

When I first came to Abyssinian, I was about twenty-two years old. I was the youth assistant to Dr. Samuel DeWitt Proctor, one of the greatest educators and theologians of the twentieth century. He was a close friend and collaborator with Dr. Martin Luther King Jr. Dr. Proctor was my mentor. I worked under him, and for him, for seventeen years.

I was a young, energetic minister, a James Brown fanatic. James Brown was my man. I used to put on my bib overalls, hook up my boom box outside the church, and dance with the kids in the middle of the street to James Brown's music. I'd quote James Brown in sermons. Still do. One of the lyrics I liked was, "Without an education you might as well be dead." And there was, "How you gonna get respect when you haven't cut your process yet?" It was fun. Music was a big part of my ministry with young people. It helped me reach them.

Back then, the seniors of the church saw me as their son. I used to have a lot more time, so Christmas morning, Thanksgiving morning, I'd run out early and visit the sick in hospitals and then run home and try to be with my family. But I can't do those things anymore. My responsibilities are just so much more heavy. I'm sad about that. I kind of liked it when I was younger and kind of the darling of the congregation. When you're the pastor, people respect you, but now you're the one who has to make the tough decisions. That has been difficult for me. But with authority comes tremendous responsibility.

I'm blessed. I'm just trying to maintain and grow a very special institution in the African world. I'm wedded to this place until the Lord calls me home—or until I reach age seventy-two, when the bylaws say I have to retire.

If I took my hat shop downtown, I could get

two, three times what I get in Harlem. But it's not about that.

I am grateful. I am content. It's like the old West Indian people say,

"Eat little and live long."

JUNIOR "BUNN" LEONARD

# Junior "Bunn" Leonard, *47*

Bunn. Since I was fourteen, that's what people call me. Bunn. A friend of mine made it up and it stuck. Mention my real name to customers, Junior Leonard, they wouldn't know who you talking about. It's Bunn. Just Bunn. Funny thing, a lot of people don't think Bunn is a person; they think it is a hat. "Is that a Bunn you're wearing?"

I've been making hats for twenty years. In the islands they say, "Go to school or learn a trade." I learned a trade. I'm from Trinidad. But people shouldn't talk about where they're from. Puts you in a box. Anyway, we all from one place: Ethiopia, the cradle, where life began in the Garden of Eden.

There's nobody who works in my shop for me. My hands make everything. My customers come in and say something like, "Look, Bunn, I'm going to this wedding. I've got an outfit and I want a hat to go with it." Then I ask what they like in a hat. "Well, I don't like the crown too high and I like the brim to dip in the front." What colors do you like? "Use cream and a bit of cinnamon." When they come back and try it on they say, "That's it, Bunn!"

That's my joy. That's my gift. I can look at you—how you walk, how you dress—and I can make a hat for you.

My hats are one-of-a-kind because my customers are one-of-a-kind. There's this lady who lives in Harlem named Aissatou. Her son was that Olympic fencer. Black kid from

Harlem competing in fencing, of all things. Aissatou's been a customer of mine since I opened. She was getting ready to travel to Sydney to see her son compete. She came by with a baseball cap in her hands and said, "Bunn, can you believe this is what they gave me to wear?"

The cap was off-white. It had a patch of the Olympic rings in the front. Your average baseball cap. It was not her style, definitely not her style. She wears long dreadlocks. She said, "Could you make me an off-white hat and put this Olympic patch on it?" I said, "Oh, I'll come up with something." She said, "Remember, I'm going to be representing. It has to say 'Harlem!'" She gave me two weeks.

For a week and a half, I'm sewing other hats and thinking, *What in the world am I going to do?* Well, I took off the patch and I took off the strap in the back. The strap said "Sydney Olympic Games." I made this crazy, unorthodox hat. There was no brim on this hat. At the base of it, it looked like the crowns Zulu women used to wear. It fit tight to the head and expanded into three lifts, three layers. I sewed the patch on the front and the strap on the back. When Aissatou came in she said, "This is it, Bunn! This is it!" When she got back from Sydney, she said people were stopping her all over the place, asking to take pictures with her and that crazy hat.

I love Harlem. If I took my hat shop downtown, I could get two, three times what I get in Harlem. But it's not about that. I am grateful. I am content. It's like the old West Indian people say, "Eat little and live long."

People don't think of fencing when they think of Harlem.

Basketball maybe, the Globetrotters. But not fencing. . . . One day,

my teacher read a newspaper article about my fencing

accomplishments to the class. The guys said,

"Oh, so you gay *and* a sellout?"

AKHNATEN SPENCER-EL

# Akhnaten Spencer-EL, *22*

People don't think of fencing when they think of Harlem. Basketball maybe, the Globetrotters. But not fencing. In high school, I tried to hide it. I was the class clown, always made fun of people. If kids found out I was a fencer, I knew I'd get it back. One day, my teacher read a newspaper article about my fencing accomplishments to the class. The guys said, "Oh, so you gay *and* a sellout?"

When I was twelve, I played Little League baseball with the Harlem Dodgers. My assistant coach, she was dating Peter Westbrook, a six-time Olympian in fencing. Peter lives in Harlem, too, and runs his own fencing club. Peter said to me, "You're fast and you have good hand-eye coordination. You'd be a good fencer."

My first competitions were in Upstate New York and Downtown Manhattan. White parents would look at me like they didn't really want me there. One time, when I was fifteen, I had twenty-five matches in a single competition and I didn't lose one. One of the white kids I beat that day said, "Look, man, you finished first but they're changing the scores so you'll finish fourth." That kid had heart.

Eventually, I got good enough to take private lessons from a Russian coach. Once you get a coach, there's no messing around because serious money is involved. And it was Peter's serious money. My coach, Yuri, and I clashed because I was just a regular Harlem boy: I didn't like anybody telling me what to do. In Russia, if you didn't listen, you got hit. And then you might be arrested by the KGB.

I remember one time, I kept doing one movement wrong. Yuri got angry and hit me on my arm with his saber. So I hit him on his hand with my saber. He couldn't believe it. He took his mask off and stared at me. He said he didn't want to work with me anymore. But Peter talked to him. Peter said, "You can't deal with kids from Harlem like you do kids from Russia. They're not afraid." Through the years, Yuri began to understand me and I understood him. Yuri really helped me.

I competed in France, Belgium, Hungary. A lot of my friends had never even been to Brooklyn. When I was eighteen, I shocked the fencing world when I was ranked the number-one junior in the world. Shocked me, too.

I was featured on Oprah's show, I was in all the newspapers, then IBM did a commercial about me. They went around Harlem and had people talk about me going to the Olympics. At Mr. Savage's barbershop, one guy said, "I didn't know brothers could fence." Well, when I went to the 2000 games in Sydney, they played that commercial 24/7. Every two minutes, people would say, "Hey, it's you! Can I have your autograph?" It was great. It was so great that I forgot I was there to compete.

When they announced my name before my first match, the crowd went crazy. They started chanting my nickname: "A-khi . . . A-khi . . . A-khi." I was too nervous. I had to fence a Chinese guy who I had beat so many times before. But I lost. Bad. Something like fifteen to seven. I was so embarrassed. Yuri said, "Don't worry about it. You'll be back." After a while, I went out to sit with my parents in the stands. I had my head down because I felt like I let everybody down. But as I walked through the stands, everyone stood and clapped. I couldn't believe it. Row after row, people clapping. My mother hugged me. She said, "I'm proud of you. You're an Olympian."

In the Riverton, we played a brand of basketball that

people would come from all over the city to see. . . . It was

about not just doing something, but doing it poetically, creatively.

It's like the tradition of "playing the dozens," where black kids

try to top one another with insults: "Your mama's so fat

she has her own zip code."

SHERMAN EDMISTON JR.

# Sherman Edmiston Jr., *65*

ART DEALER

People overlook how integral basketball is to the Harlem experience. Everybody knows about the Harlem Globetrotters, but not many people know about the Rens. They were the precursors to the Globetrotters. During the Harlem Renaissance, the Rens played before spectators at the Renaissance Ballroom on 138th Street and Seventh Avenue. By the time I was coming up, the Rens were defunct. But three members of the Rens taught me to play basketball: Dollie King, who was one of the first blacks to play professional basketball; Pop Gates, who also became a Globetrotter; and Puggy Bell, who was in charge of security at the Riverton projects, where I grew up.

The Riverton is a group of buildings on 135th Street to 138th Street, from Fifth Avenue to Madison Avenue. The Riverton was built for black residents after the Second World War. Not just anyone could get in, only middle-class families, people on the move. David Dinkins, the former mayor of New York City, grew up at the Riverton. So did Sharon DuPont, who became the head of Motown. Clifford Alexander Sr. was the general manager of the Riverton. His son, Clifford Jr., went on to become the first black Secretary of the Army. The Riverton was a big deal at the time. Black people even came to the Riverton to commit suicide. They'd go to the top and jump. Thirteen floors. It was the thing to do.

Kids in the Riverton learned to play basketball from the old Rens: Puggy Bell, Dollie King, and Pop Gates. They were incredible ballplayers. They dribbled between the legs; they passed behind the back. Very flamboyant. Black ball, as they say. The way they would teach you was to get you on the court and beat the hell out of you. They'd throw elbows, knock you down, stomp on you. They were great teachers. There was no, "Okay, kid, keep your head up when you dribble." No, you learned by watching how they drove to the basket, how they looked left and passed right, how they faked a shot and left a guy hanging in the air. We learned by playing with them.

In the Riverton, we played a brand of basketball that people would come from all over the city to see. We'd go from the Riverton courts to 152nd and Amsterdam Avenue, a court we called Battleground. It meant exactly what it said. And then there was a big court at the Harlem River projects. What you see today in the NBA, it came from those courts. It was all the stuff that white coaches in school would say, "Don't do that!" But that's what we did. It was all about style. It was about not just doing something, but doing it poetically, creatively. It's like the tradition of "playing the dozens," where black kids try to top one another with insults: "Your mama's so fat she has her own zip code." What can I tell you? It's a black thing.

I was not that tall, so my shot was the hook shot because it's hard to block. One time, I threw a hook shot from the corner with my left hand, in the face of Charlie Riley. Charlie was a big guy with hands like shovels. Spectators went, "Wooo! Ohhh! In yo' *face*, Charlie!" That was so sweet.

We were toughened on the courts. The key to it all was you had to have guts. You had to be willing to get knocked around to learn the game. That's true on the courts. That's true in life.

Our house was built in 1888 for James Anthony Bailey,

who was co-owner of the Barnum and Bailey Circus. . . . It was

built for about fifty thousand dollars. You can't build

a driveway for that amount now.

WARREN BLAKE

## Warren Blake, *77, with wife Marguerite*

OWNERS OF LANDMARK HOUSE

Our house was built in 1888 for James Anthony Bailey, who was co-owner of the Barnum and Bailey Circus. The design was considered flamboyant in its time, with the stained-glass windows and the tower, but I don't think it looks flamboyant today. It has three floors, five bedrooms, fourteen-foot high ceilings, a solarium. It was built for about fifty thousand dollars. You can't build a driveway for that amount now.

In 1943, my wife was the youngest woman in the state to hold a funeral director's license. She was twenty-one. By 1950, she was tired of working for other people and she started looking for a place to open her own funeral home. She knocked on the door of her dream house, the Bailey House, which at the time was owned by a German doctor named Koempel. I learned recently that Dr. Koempel helped found a fraternal organization named the Steuben Society in this house. Anyhow, when Dr. Koempel's wife opened the door my wife said, "If you ever decide to sell this house, please sell it to me." Mrs. Koempel must have wondered who this bold black woman was at her door. But it was meant to be. Later that year, the house was put up for sale. We bought it and my wife opened the M. Marshall Blake Funeral Home. The "M" stands for "Marguerite," my wife's name. In those days, people felt more comfortable doing business with a man so she went with the "M." People assumed I was the "M," but it was always her.

We always thought it was an impressive house in an impressive neighborhood: Sugar Hill. Six sitting judges lived in the neighborhood. Right around the corner is the 409 Edgecomb apartment building. W. E. B. DuBois used to live there. He started the NAACP.

Thurgood Marshall, the Supreme Court Justice, lived there. They used to say you'd wipe out black leadership for a generation if you dropped a bomb on 409.

The funeral home is on the middle floor of the house, we do our embalming in the solarium, and we live upstairs. We've had films and TV shows made here. About fifteen years ago, Katharine Hepburn shot *Grace Quigley* here with Nick Nolte. It was a dark comedy about murder. About six o'clock every morning, before they started shooting, Katharine Hepburn would come in and call upstairs for Marguerite. "Oh Mar-gue-rite. Morning." She and Marguerite would sit on the bottom step in the foyer and drink coffee and talk.

We have a china cabinet in the house. It's filled with cremated ashes going all the way back to 1954. Superstitious people left the urns with us. They'd say, "We don't want to wake up in the middle of the night and find uncle so-and-so hovering over us." They'd say, "We don't want no 'haints' in the house." We have about twenty urns and I can say for a fact that there are no haints in this house. I remember, we used to have a mirror over the fireplace in the room where we put caskets for viewing. And do you know that we had to cover that mirror because people were afraid that the image of the dead person would appear in it.

Not a week passes without downtown realtors asking if we want to sell. Reverend Moon's people offered us over a million dollars. But we'll never sell. People always ask how we feel living in a city landmark. We feel great because it's paid for.

From the moment you come to the

United States, even if you don't know the language,

you know there are only two colors here:

white and not-white.

AURORA FLORES

# Aurora Flores, 48

PUBLIC RELATIONS CONSULTANT

One black guy got mad at me once and he told me I should go back to Puerto Rico where I came from. I said, "Well, honey, I wasn't born in Puerto Rico. I was born in East Harlem." He said, "You Spanish people always want to pass for white." I said, "There's a difference between passing and surviving."

Mongo Santamaria, the great jazz congo player from Cuba, he is very black. When you look at him you see Africa. Mongo came to the United States in the fifties. He was doing a concert tour in the South. There was an accident with the bus and his leg was injured severely. He was taken to a segregated hospital and they were going to put him in the "Colored" section. He didn't speak English, so through his interpreter he asked, "What will happen to me if I go to the 'Colored' section?" They said, "They'll amputate your leg." He said, "And what will happen to me in the 'White' section?" They said, "Oh, they'll bring you a real doctor and maybe he can save your leg." He said, "Wait, wait, I'm not colored. I'm Cuban."

Well, Mongo convinced them to put him in the White section and they saved his leg. Now, is that passing or is that surviving? From the moment you come to the United States, even if you don't know the language, you know there are only two colors here: white and not-white.

I have always been intrigued by language, how it divides and unites people. Right on 116th Street, there's a place called La Marqueta. In the late fifties, when I was seven or eight, that was the only place you could come to get tropical fruits and vegetables: coconuts, green bananas, yucca, that kind of stuff. There was always a stench of fish in that place. My mother and I would go there twice a week. She and the men in aprons would speak in Spanish.

Along the street, there were stores that sold clothes and other items. Almost all of the merchants were Orthodox Jews. They had the little black suits with the black hats and the curls. But they didn't speak Spanish like at La Marqueta.

My mother found out that the Jewish merchants had a tradition that if you were the first customer of the day, they had to sell you an item at the price you wanted. If they didn't, it would be bad luck and they wouldn't sell much the rest of the day.

Very early one Saturday morning, my mother and I went to this one store near La Marqueta, where my mother had been eyeing some winter coats. Being the eldest, I was the family translator, the "go between." My mother told me to ask the vendor for his price for the coats. When I told her she got angry because she had gone in there the week before and they were cheaper. She says, "*¿El está loco, o que?*" Is he nuts? She says we're the first customers and he's got to give the coats to her at the price she wants. She was yelling. Her arms were flailing. She says, "*Dile que el es un bandido.*" Tell him he's a thief. "*Dile! Dile!*" Tell him! Tell him!

I was so nervous. I turned to the man and said, calmly, "My mommy said . . . she would like a better price." The man smiled at me, a knowing kind of smile. He said, "You're a smart little girl. I'm going to give you these coats at the price your mother wants. And when you grow up, you can come back and work for me anytime you want."

A fine wardrobe used to count for something.

On Sundays, black people would dress to the nines

and stroll up and down Seventh Avenue,

even if they had nowhere to go.

DENA HILL MORRISON

# Dena Hill Morrison, *82*

RETIRED SOCIAL WORKER

I was a teenager when I first came to Harlem. That was September of 1940. My father had just died and my mother told me it was time for me to leave because she thought somebody was going to kill me. You see, I grew up in Houston, Mississippi, and didn't take lip from anybody. If a white man said, "Get off the street, nigger," I'd say, "*You* get off the street." My father raised us to be proud, stand tall, never say, "I can't." My father used to say, "My kids lift their heads to God and bow to no one."

When I first moved to New York, I didn't live in Harlem. A family in Long Island had sent me a ticket to come live with them, be their housekeeper. They had a very bad little boy, Billy, and couldn't find anyone in *all* of New York willing to work for them. [*Laughs.*]

On my days off, Thursdays and every other Sunday, I'd catch the train to Harlem. My older sister, Wilma, lived on 148th Street near St. Nicholas Avenue, the Sugar Hill area. Black people used to say, "That's where all the uppity niggas live, on Sugar Hill." The renowned soprano Dorothy Maynor lived here; they never did let her sing at Lincoln Center. Nat King Cole's aunt lived around the corner; he dressed for his wedding at her house. The CEO of a major company had a black mistress up the street. I won't name names because that company is still in business, but a big black limousine would pull up and whisk her off. It was so expensive to live on Sugar Hill that people said we ate corn flakes to pay the rent. When I moved into my building fifty years ago, my rent was six dollars a week. Lord, have mercy! That was a lot of corn flakes.

Sugar Hill was beautiful. Everyone had flowers in their yards, every building had a doorman in uniform. Decorum meant something in those days. One time, a woman put a pot of collards on her windowsill. Neighbors yelled up from the street: "Take that pot out of the window! We don't do that round here." She was new to the neighborhood.

We worked so hard that it meant a lot to get all dressed up and go dancing. Places like the Cotton Club were off limits. They had black entertainers, like Duke Ellington, but no black customers. No, we'd go to the Rockland Palace, Renaissance, the Savoy, the Rainbow Room, Golden Gate, Small's Paradise. You couldn't get into some of the dinner dances unless you wore formal attire. A fine wardrobe used to count for something. On Sundays, black people would dress to the nines and stroll up and down Seventh Avenue, even if they had nowhere to go.

One time, the guy I was seeing, Stuart, he came to pick me up for a dance at the Renaissance on 138th and Seventh Avenue. Stuart had on a white zoot suit, like Cab Calloway used to wear, white shoes that were pointed at the toe, a white hat, white shirt, and blue tie. A gold chain was attached to the coat and hung down below his knee. He rattled all the way up the stairs. My friends said Stuart couldn't come with us dressed like that. They said, "They won't let you in without formal attire." The rest of us had on gowns and tuxedos. Stuart got angry. He said, "I'm from Chicago and we're two steps ahead of *everybody* in Harlem." He looked at me and said, "You think you're too cute for me, anyway."

That was the last time I saw Stuart. Went to the dance without him. Had a good time, too.

All a guy needed to go to the Savoy

was a ticket; the Thursday girls would foot the expense

of drinks and food. They had the money.

JAMES ALLEN

# James Allen, *76*

EXECUTIVE DIRECTOR OF A DRUG
TREATMENT PROGRAM

When I was nineteen or twenty, I traveled up and down the West Coast, from San Francisco to San Diego, playing my guitar in clubs. It was an acoustic guitar. There were no electric guitars back then. Seems like that guitar was always in my arms. My girl, Mary Elizabeth, traveled with me. She was my first love. They were all I had, Mary Elizabeth and my guitar.

Sometimes I had to travel without Mary Elizabeth. I'd tell my best friend to take care of my lady—which he did. They started a relationship. It devastated me. I guess you'd say I became a vagabond, moving around the country with no real purpose or plan. Eventually, I headed for the end of the world: New York City.

I first arrived at the Capital Bus terminal on 50th and Eighth. That was in 1948. I stayed in the terminal for a week, playing my guitar and trying to figure out where black people lived. I'd walk up to white people and say, "Where do the colored people live?" They looked at me like I was crazy. One day, an old white lady said, "Mister, what you do is go down to such-and-such place. At five o'clock, you'll see everybody getting on trains. Whichever train the most colored people get on, you take that train." That's what I did.

I got off on 145th and Lenox. I'd never in my life seen as many black people in one place. I grew up in Lingo, Louisiana. Down south, black people could only go to county fairs on a certain day: Colored People's Day. It was usually the last day—right before the fair left for the next town. So when I got off that subway and saw so many black people, I thought I had stumbled upon Colored People's Day at the fair or something. If you were a loner like me, Harlem was the perfect place to hide.

I got a job pressing clothes and got a room for a dollar and a quarter a week. I kept to myself because my heart was still in this deep hole. My guitar kept me from going up the walls over Mary Elizabeth. After work, I'd play myself to sleep.

One night, a newly found friend said, "I know what's wrong with you." He said he was going to take me somewhere and we had to get dressed up. In those days, a man wasn't dressed unless he had on a suit and tie, overcoat and gloves, and a hat. But I didn't wear hats because hats gave me a headache.

My friend took me to the Savoy Ballroom. The Savoy was something else! You could hear all the great bands: Erskine Hawkins, Lester Young, Count Basie. You could dance and meet girls. All a guy needed to go to the Savoy was a ticket; the Thursday girls would foot the expense of drinks and food. They had the money. Most of them were domestic workers and looked forward to their days off: Thursdays and every other Sunday. The Thursday girls at the Savoy helped me forget Mary Elizabeth.

Things have changed so much, but I still think Harlem is the greatest place in the world to live. For forty years, I've run a rehabilitation center for drug addicts. My role in Harlem is to pick up the pieces of people broken by drugs. That's my role. My dream?

I want to play the guitar.

When I told the principal I wanted to teach at her school, she said, "You're male, you're white, and you're from the South. You have a few things working against you."

RON CLARK

# Ron Clark, 30

TEACHER

One night, I saw a program on TV about schools in Harlem. At the time, I was a teacher in a rural town in North Carolina. The show said that very bright kids in Harlem end up with low test scores because it's so difficult to keep good teachers. I felt like I had a calling. The next day, I talked to my co-teacher. I said, "Barbara, I'm going to go teach in Harlem." She said, "Are you crazy?" I saw that TV show on a Wednesday night of the last week of school. That Monday, I drove up to Harlem. I didn't have a place to stay, I didn't know anybody, I just drove up in my little Honda Accord and got a room at the YMCA.

Then every day I went from school to school to talk to the principals. When I got to P.S. 83, I walked in on a fight between a sixth-grader and a male aide. I helped break it up and sat with the student to calm him down. I asked him what happened and why he responded that way, and I listened with genuine interest. After about fifteen minutes, he said, "If there were more teachers like you at this school, maybe I wouldn't get in trouble." I said to myself, *That's a sign. This is where I'm supposed to be.*

When I told the principal I wanted to teach at her school, she said, "You're male, you're white, and you're from the South. You have a few things working against you." She said, "If you want the job, I'm going to give you the most challenging class I have. They have a lot of discipline problems and they're not working at grade level." I said, "I want them."

I was a little nervous so I got a list of all the kids' addresses and went around to all the homes that summer to meet them and their parents. I gave them my discipline plan, a list of fifty-five rules and expectations: No "yeahs" and "nopes." We work on offering a firm handshake and on how to react if someone steps on your foot, things like that. The parents were a little shocked to see me, but they could tell I was interested in their children so they were all for it.

I thought my visits would make it easy when school started, but it wasn't easy. Some of the kids had abandonment issues with teachers who would stay for a couple of months and leave, so they tested me. But I ate lunch with them every day. I spent time with them after school. I took them on field trips, just anything to show them I wasn't going anywhere. I even tried to learn to jump double Dutch. When those two ropes start turning, it's like jumping into a blender. I just about broke my neck! It took me three months to pick it up. The first time I got in, I stayed for thirty seconds. The kids were going crazy, laughing and screaming. It helped me reach them. At the end of the year, my fifth-graders had higher test scores than the gifted sixth-grade students!

Some people say if you can touch just one child, it's worth every sacrifice. That's the total opposite of my philosophy. We can't afford to touch just one child. We have to touch them all.

I think a lot of people have a misconception about Harlem. They would be shocked to see it through my eyes. I find Harlem is a wonderfully cultural place with parents who care about education and students who want to learn.

I'm no savior. I'm just a teacher.

For thirty-three years, I've run a skills-training institute. We're based in the Theresa Towers, which used to be the famous Hotel Theresa before it became an office building in 1970.

ELSIE SIMMONS

# Elsie Simmons, *60*

CEO OF EMC ENTERPRISES

Hardly a day goes by when someone on 125th Street doesn't say, "Hi, Miss Simmons. Remember me? Guess what I'm doing now." For thirty-three years, I've run a skills-training institute. We're based in the Theresa Towers, which used to be the famous Hotel Theresa before it became an office building in 1970. We started out training legal secretaries then we moved into computer training. Something like thirteen thousand students have come through here. We have students who've gone on to become lawyers, teachers. But we can't reach everybody. I was more idealistic before, but now I realize there's such a thing as being so damaged that you can't be fixed.

In 1982, we had a lot of trouble with one young man. Let's say his name was Richard. He had just been released from juvenile detention. They had to let him go because he had reached eighteen.

Richard was not well socialized. He didn't know how to befriend anyone. Emotionally, he was just flat—unless he got angry. Richard had a very bad temper and sometimes it seemed like he'd just as soon kill you as say hello. He would suppress it as much as he could, but it was always there, his rage. You could feel it. You could feel him seethe. I was afraid of him.

At the same time, there was something about Richard. Something sad. On the other side of his anger, you sensed that there was a human being wanting to connect. But he couldn't find his way.

I keep a consulting psychologist on staff. One day, the psychologist met with Richard. She came into my office and said to me, "I think you need to hear this." I went into her office and asked Richard if he wanted to tell me something. He said, "I've been on the streets of New York since the age of eight. My mother moved to Albany and left me here. She took my brothers and sisters, but she left me."

I couldn't even imagine my parents not being in my world at eight or how an eight-year-old could survive on the streets of New York. I still can't imagine it. I asked him how he survived. He said, "I killed people. For money." He said, "I just wanted to tell you." I told him, "I don't need to know that type of information, but if you share it, and if it's true, I have to report it."

For some reason, Richard connected with me. Normally, I don't interact with many students. But I said, "Let's go for a walk. Let's walk down Fifth Avenue." Richard said, "Fifth Avenue? I couldn't walk on Fifth Avenue." I said, "Why not?" He said, "Only white people walk on Fifth Avenue." I said, "Okay, where are you comfortable walking?" He said, "I'm comfortable in a four-block area around where I live. That's where I walk." He was living in a room by himself. I sensed that something very bad was going to happen to Richard.

The psychologist thought it might be helpful if we got him to reconnect with his mother. A couple of weeks later we found her in Albany, and we arranged for him to go see her on a weekend. But when he got there, she changed her mind. His mother wouldn't see him. After that, we never saw Richard again.

Real damage. That's real damage.

I go back to my village once a year.

They say, "Moctar, we miss you. Why you don't come back?"

I say, "When you live somewhere for a long time, you belong

to that place. I belong to Harlem now."

MOCTAR YARA

# Moctar Yara, *34*

STORE OWNER

Maybe it happens once a month. Usually, it's kids that do it, black kids. They open the door of our store and shout something rude about Africans and then they disappear into the crowd on 125th Street. It bothers my wife, but I tell her it's nothing. Those kids don't know what Africa is about, and they don't want to know. They're young.

Djema is the name of my store. We make robes for church choirs. For hotels, we make bed covers, pillows. We also make dresses, shower curtains, anything you want. Djema is also the name of my village in Mali. I go back to my village once a year. They say, "Moctar, we miss you. Why you don't come back?" I say, "When you live somewhere for a long time, you belong to that place. I belong to Harlem now."

I began as a vendor on 125th street. There were a lot street vendors back then. Africans, Jamaicans, African Americans. We were selling CDs, clothes, food, art, everything you can think of. But the people who owned the stores wanted us to move. They said we block the street and steal their customers. But it wasn't true. People used to buy from the vendors outside, then they buy from the stores inside. Everybody made a little money. But in 1994, Mayor Giuliani said he wanted to clean Harlem, and he started with us. He said vendors must move to a market on 116th Street. Myself, I didn't believe it was going to happen because people liked shopping with us.

Back then, I lived in an apartment on 125th Street. At midnight one night, I heard some noise. I looked outside my window and there were hundreds of police. From 125th between Lenox and Seventh and up to 126th, everything was full with police cars, police horses, police dogs. I had never seen that much police in my life. They had on their riot masks and clubs. I said, "My God! Tomorrow it's going to be war."

The police waited all night to see who would come to try to set up their table, but nobody showed up. Everybody in the African community began to call each other. We decided not to go out there because we were so scared. There were so many police with nobody to fight. No one went out there for weeks, weeks with so many police and no business. The city set up a new place on 116th Street and some of us went to look at it. But I told myself, *It's ruined.*

Some vendors moved to Chicago and Detroit, some moved to Brooklyn, and some just gave up and found a job. But a lot of the stores went out of business, too. When the vendors left 125th Street, customers wondered what happen and they just keep on walking.

I went to 116th Street for four years. But I'm back on 125th Street, and I'm in a store now. If this building was owned by a white man, I'd probably be gone by now. But it's owned by a black man. He could make big money if he put me out tomorrow, but he rents to me. And I'm working hard so when the chance comes maybe I can buy it.

In Mali, the families are very close. If you have a hundred dollars, it's not yours. It belongs to the whole family. That's the only way the family is going to be successful. And that's the way I see Harlem now. If we don't stick together, we're not going to make it.

$I$ like abstract art.

Maybe because it's something like me. You look at it

and you think you know what you see, but what you see

might not be what it is.

CAROL ANNE MARTIN

# Carol Anne Martin, *52*

ASSISTANT AT STUDIO MUSEUM IN HARLEM

People look at my appearance, and hear how much I talk, and they think I'm this bold person. But I'm not. I don't have a college education and that makes me feel inferior. That's not easy to admit, but it's true. A friend told me, "Look, I know some real idiots with Ph.D.'s." I said, "Well, I don't."

I had never been around a bunch of educated black people until I came to work for the Studio Museum as a clerk. I was twenty-nine and *real* ignorant. Knew nothing about black culture. We had three people in the Artists-in-Residence Program when I came here. The artists stay for a year and the museum gives them studio space and a stipend and an exhibition. That year, 1979, the artists in residence were Jacqui Holmes, Louis Delsarte, and Candace Hill-Montgomery. On breaks and after hours, I would go talk to them: "What made you want to become an artist?" "God, I can't even draw. How can you do that?"

One day, I saw a simple piece Candace Hill-Montgomery had brought with her. It was a three-foot-long pipe, like a plumbing pipe, with a hinge and a piece of cloth wrapped around it. The cloth was black and white, like a flag. I said, "That's really, really nice." She said, "Oh, it's just a piece I did." I said, "I'd like to buy that." She looked up at me and said, "Are you serious?" I said, "Yeah! How much do you want for it?" She said, "Oh, I don't know. How about fifty dollars?" Of course, today I realize that she was practically giving it to me. But back then I was shocked. I was only making eight thousand dollars a year. I said, "Let me think about it."

Well, when I got my next paycheck, I gave Candice fifty dollars for the artwork. That fifty dollars came out of my rent money. I made up a good story for my roommate, Diana, and told her I'd pay her back. So I had to hide the piece under my bed. Then one of my big-mouth friends came over and said, "Carol, where's that artwork you bought?" Diana said, "Artwork? What artwork?" It all came out. Diana was pissed but she got over it.

My second piece of art, I got it when the museum had a grab bag one Christmas. David Hammons pulled my name. David Hammons wasn't David Hammons back then. He was an artist in residence, but now he's one of the most noted artists in Harlem. Some of his works sell for hundreds of thousands of dollars.

The grab-bag gift David made was a wire clothing hanger that he pulled open and covered with little fibers of human hair, and at the bottom is a little circle of linoleum that's pink and white. He put little holes in the linoleum and tied tea bags to them. You can hook the hanger on the edge of a table and the linoleum will swing like a pendulum. I was just so happy. I asked him, I said, "David, so what happens when the tea bags fall apart?" He said, "You put some more tea bags on there." I said, "Oh, okay."

Over the years, I've purchased pieces from Russell Hamilton, Janet Henry, Terry Boddie, Emilio Cruz, and other artists in residence. Many of them were very open about themselves, and when I looked at their work I could see the person—even though the art was abstract.

I like abstract art. Maybe because it's something like me. You look at it and you think you know what you see, but what you see might not be what it is.

I got my medical degree from Howard University

in 1937. People felt that a woman studying medicine

was a waste of time and money because women wouldn't practice;

they would only get married and have babies. I eventually got

married and had babies, but I went back to my practice.


MURIEL PETIONI

# Muriel Petioni, M.D., *87*

PHYSICIAN

My father was from Trinidad, a British colony. He was a journalist who wrote articles very critical of British colonialism. They told him he'd better leave. So by 1918 he decided to come to New York and study medicine. He told my mother he'd try to send for us a year later, once he got settled. My mother was from Guyana. She said, "A year's plenty. I'm coming over whether you're settled or not."

My father worked at the New York shipyards, which paid a lot of money. At night, he went to City College and later he went to Howard University for his medical degree. We got an apartment and we brought relatives over and they helped pay the rent. Mama worked in the garment industry as a finisher. She did that until my father completed medical school, then she became his receptionist. That was in 1925.

After my father practiced a year or two, he bought a brownstone on 131st. He had an office in the house, as did many of the doctors of that day. I was twelve at the time. I would open the door for patients. That was during Prohibition, when it was illegal to drink alcohol. If a patient needed alcohol for medical purposes, the doctor would give the patient a government coupon and they would turn it in to get the alcohol. One day, this patient came in looking for my father. I told him my father wasn't in. The man said, "Can I have a glass of water?" When I went to get the water, he went through my father's desk and stole the coupon book. We never saw him again.

My father told me I could do *anything* I wanted to do. I had no particular talents, so by age twelve I decided that becoming a doctor was what I wanted to do. I got my medical degree from Howard University in 1937. People felt that a woman studying medicine was a waste of time and money because women wouldn't practice; they would only get married and have babies. I eventually got married and had babies, but I went back to my practice.

Harlem Hospital was one of the few white hospitals that always took a few black interns, so I applied and got a spot. We were paid twenty dollars a month. I was twenty-three and really quite shy but my father said, "Don't be awed by *anyone*. You have a medical degree just like any other doctor."

The first six months of my internship were spent riding the ambulance. A call came in one day saying a woman was about to deliver a baby in her apartment. I said, "I don't know anything about delivering a baby." The driver got a kick out of that. The drivers weren't medically trained, but they had a lot of practical experience. The driver said, "Oh, don't worry. I'll help you do it." Luckily, nature took over pretty much: The woman pushed and I caught. That was my first delivery. I think I was more anxious than the mother.

When I started my private practice, a lot of black people thought white folks knew more about medicine, particularly if they were Jewish. People would talk on and on about going up to see the Jewish doctors on 145th Street. And a lot of men were embarrassed to visit a woman doctor. In those days, I'd say two-thirds of my patients were women. One of my male patients said his friends teased him about seeing a woman doctor. He said to me, "But I don't care. You're a good doctor."

I was raised in Harlem.

Born in Harlem Hospital. My first address was

498 West 124th Street. There're projects there now.

LUTHER GALES

# Luther Gales, *61*

HOUSING POLICE OFFICER (RETIRED)

I was raised in Harlem. Born in Harlem Hospital. My first address was 498 West 124th Street. There're projects there now. In the late fifties, I moved up to Harlem River projects up on 151st Street, the first projects in Harlem. Later on, I worked there. I was a New York City Housing Police Officer. We had the same powers of regular police officers, but our jurisdiction was the housing projects. I went in in 1965.

That was a dangerous job. One night—a cold, cold night—a young man pulled a knife on some people. He thought he was a ninja. He had on these long, black robes. My partner and I found him and I put him up against a wall. My partner had his gun on him. As I'm searching his upper body, I find a long spear. A spear, right? Then I find one of those circular stars you see them throw in the karate movies. I can't believe this guy. I squatted down and started patting his legs and I find a knife in his boots. This guy ain't right in the head.

I had my gloves off so I'm thinking about how cold my hands are. When it's cold I'm useless. Apparently, the ninja also had a hatchet hidden in all those robes. I missed it. He evidently thought he was fast as Bruce Lee or something because while I was patting his legs, he pulled the hatchet and turned to strike me. My partner shot him twice. BAM! BAM! He was paralyzed. Had to get around in a wheelchair. Fool almost got himself killed. Almost split my head open, too.

———

I lost my job over facial hair. I had let my mustache grow into a beard. My captain said, "Luther, you got to shave that off." I said, "Captain, it ain't bothering nobody." He said, "Rules are rules. You got to shave it off." The guidebook did say that beards were unacceptable. The next morning I shaved it off, but I didn't feel good about it. For black men, facial hair is a cultural thing. I was looking in the mirror at this naked face and I started thinking, *Muhammad Ali took a stand and refused to serve in Viet Nam. Malcolm X and H. Rap Brown and Stokely Carmichael took a stand. I'm just an armchair revolutionary wearing a badge.* There was this feeling of militancy and pride in Harlem, but I wasn't involved. I started crying.

Within thirty days, I grew my beard back. And I told myself, *I'm not shaving.* I was suspended and then I was terminated. I was out of work for ten months. I'm driving a cab to bring some money in. But my wife and I have four kids and she's pissed off. I told my wife that I'd read somewhere that a slave ain't supposed to die a natural death. She said, "You better get back on that job or *I'll* kill you!" I said, "I ain't going back. I'm *militant.*" She said, "Militant don't put food on the table." All my friends said, "You a fool. You a fool. They want you back but you got to shave." I said, "I ain't shaving."

Before long, it turned into this big thing. Gil Noble mentioned it on his television show. The papers picked up on it. It kept mushrooming. I'm walking around wearing a dashiki and a beard and everybody knows me: Officer Militant.

They tried to compromise. They said they'd hire me back if I cut it off. I said no. They hired me back anyway, and rescinded the rule. Two days later I shaved it all off.

In February of 2000, I was on a beach in Mexico

with my daughter Lise. . . . I said, "You know what, Lise? I'm moving

to Harlem." She said, "You're what?" I said, "I'm moving to Harlem."

She said, "Can we finish our vacation first?"

CLARA VILLAROSA

# Clara Villarosa, *70*

BOOKSTORE OWNER

In February of 2000, I was on a beach in Mexico with my daughter Lise. Lise and my other daughter, Linda, live in Brooklyn. At the time, I lived in Denver. I had a bookstore there, but I was ready to sell the store, retire, and move to Brooklyn to be near my daughters and grandchildren. Lise and I were sitting in hammocks when it hit me. I said, "You know what, Lise? I'm moving to Harlem." She said, "You're what?" I said, "I'm moving to Harlem." She said, "Can we finish our vacation first?"

When I made that decision, it never occurred to me that I would be opening a bookstore in Harlem. I was still burned out from the first one. It was called Hue-Man. In the beginning, I couldn't get middle-class blacks to come in. So I said, *What do they value? They value the biggest and the best: houses, cars, clothing.* So I decided to tell customers that they were inside the *largest* black bookstore in the world.

My daughter Linda, said, "But Mom, you can't say that. It may not be true." I said, "It's the largest one I ever I saw." She said, "Well, how do you know there isn't one larger?" I said, "Well, I don't know. That's the point." So I started telling that to customers and they would say, "Oh, this is great! Wow, right here in Denver!"

Not long after that, Linda was at a party in New York. One of her friends said, "Linda, didn't you use to live in Denver?" She said, "Yes." Her friend said, "I was just there and I visited the largest black bookstore in the world." Linda called me in the middle of the night. She said, "Mom, it's working."

People began to hold me in high regard. Maya Angelou was on the "Today Show" and Bryant Gumbel asked her where she buys books. She said, "At Hue-Man in Denver, Colorado. It's the largest black bookstore in the world."

The publishers all believed it. Colin Powell came in for a book-signing event. Terry McMillan came when she was an unknown. She was promoting her first book, *Mama*. She also read the first two chapters of a book that hadn't been published yet: *Disappearing Acts*. I said, "Honey, I don't know who you are, but you're sitting on a gold mine there." James Baldwin came the year before he died. He asked his publisher if he could do a book signing at a black bookstore. Of course, they had to send him to the largest in the world.

Journalists would call me for quotes. They still call me. A reporter called the other day and asked, she said, "Do you think blacks will buy President Clinton's book?" I said, "Some will buy it, but it would *really* sell if Monica Lewinsky had been black." But I will certainly have a big display of Clinton's book because he's my neighbor. His Harlem office is two and a half blocks from my store.

At one point I said, *Oh, my God! I'm an impostor*. Apple Book Center in Detroit, Esowon in Los Angeles, Emma Rogers's store in Dallas—I'm sure they were larger. But I had become so prominent in the industry that no one wanted to tell the queen she had no clothes. In all these years, nobody ever said it wasn't true.

I want to be part of Harlem's rich literary history. That's why I'm opening my bookstore here. Of course, I'm going to call it the largest black bookstore in the world. And this time it'll be true.

I told him how unhappy I was

with my job. I told him I used to be a presser.

He said, "Girl, you can make good money

in Harlem being a presser."

JEANETTE PEPPER

# Jeanette Pepper, 56

CO-OWNER OF DRY CLEANERS

My partner, Errol Joseph, and me, we have owned our own dry cleaners for four years, but I've been in the business since I was nineteen. It was my first job. No, my first job was working as a housekeeper. I had finished high school in Greenville, South Carolina, and I couldn't afford to go to college. But when I got pregnant I knew I needed a better job than housekeeping. One month after Ron was born, I went looking. My mother said, "You just can't pop up and go to work after birthing a child." But my mind was set because I didn't have a door to shut or a pot to piss in.

They offered me a job pressing clothes at One-Hour Martinizing. I worked there for two years. Then I saw an ad in the paper: "Girls from South Needed." The ad said families in New Jersey would pay you one hundred and fifty dollars a week to take care of their children and cook. The most I ever made was seventy dollars a week. The families would even pay your bus fare. I made a plan: I was going to leave my son with my mother and send for him after two months.

That bus ride was so long. Eighteen hours. Then, when I got my pay, the family deducted the cost of my bus fare. I told them that the ad said that they were going to pay my fare. They said, "We did pay your fare, but you have to pay us back."

I had met a young man who lived in Harlem. We would go to the movies. I told him how unhappy I was with my job. I told him I used to be a presser. He said, "Girl, you can make good money in Harlem being a presser." He took me to a dry cleaners between Park and Madison. The owner, Morrie, who was Jewish, he gave me a few pieces to test my skills: a sweater, a dress, pleated pants. When I finished, a black guy named Walter came over. Walter looked at the pieces and he said, "He's gonna offer you a salary. Do *not* take it. You're good. You're fast. You can make more money doing piece work." I said, "I never heard of piece work. I want a salary." He rubbed the back of his hand and said, "Listen, we got the same skin. Trust me. Don't take it, even if he offers you two hundred and fifty dollars." I said, "Two hundred and fifty dollars!" Walter said, "Shhh! I know you didn't make much money down South, but tell him you want piece work. Two garments for seventeen cents." I said, "Seventeen cents!? I can't make no money like that." Walter said, "Trust me."

Walter went up front and Morrie came back. He looked at my work and said, "I'll start you at two hundred and twenty-five dollars a week." I said, "No, I want to go on piece work." He smiled and said, "Okay." That was a Wednesday. I quit my job in New Jersey and worked at the cleaners Thursday, Friday, and Saturday. I got paid one hundred and twenty-five dollars for only three days' work. I could have kissed Walter. I counted those bills so many times that I rubbed the green off them.

That was in July. Come September, the cleaners was closed for Labor Day. I took the train back to Greenville and got my son.

. . . More than thirty Harlem playgrounds

have been repaired or redesigned, with parents

volunteering much of the labor.


BARBARA BARLOW

# Barbara Barlow, M.D., *63*

A mother was cooking dinner for her son, who was four. He was playing in the kitchen while she cooked. It was a hot summer. The mother had the door to the apartment open, trying to get a breeze from the window in the stairwell. Her son wandered out into the stairwell and, somehow, fell out of the window. Four floors. The mother ran to the hospital with her son in her arms. He had severe head injures, and a ruptured spleen and liver. We couldn't save him. He was her only child.

That happened in 1975, when I first came to Harlem Hospital to start a pediatric surgery program. Back then, Harlem was a treacherous place for children. Children got hit by cars because they opened fire hydrants and played in the water in the middle of the street. Children got caught in the crossfire of shoot-outs because playgrounds were used for selling drugs. And when it got hot every summer, children would just be raining out the windows. I was horrified.

Each year, about three hundred children were admitted to Harlem Hospital with severe injuries. And sixty-six percent of the children who died of injuries never even came to the hospital. They were just pronounced dead at the scene.

As a pediatric surgeon, it was my job to treat injured children. But I said, *If I can't do something to prevent these injuries, I can't keep treating them because it's too depressing.* The first thing we did was help the city promote a program called "Children Can't Fly." My staff passed out thousands of balloons, bumper stickers, brochures that warned parents about the danger of open windows. We also informed parents about an ordinance requiring landlords to install window gates. Falls from windows have been reduced by ninety-six percent.

After that campaign, we worked on improving playgrounds. In 1980, I hired a staff of Harlem mothers, women invested in making things better for kids. We planned to survey the community block by block to plot out the playgrounds at schools and parks. But we couldn't find any maps of Harlem. Even the maps in taxi cabs cut off at 110th Street. We eventually got a map from the city's real estate office and photographed playgrounds park by park, school by school, until we had a photo essay of every play space in the community. Our report showed broken swings, rusted slides, shattered glass, empty crack vials. We sent the report to the mayor, the department of parks, school principals, everywhere. It got their attention.

Since then, more than thirty Harlem playgrounds have been repaired or redesigned, with parents volunteering much of the labor. Also, kids don't have to open fire hydrants in the summer anymore because we have sprinklers in the parks that cut on when it hits eighty-five degrees. The hospital has also collaborated with community groups to create arts and sports programs. By 1998, we had reduced major injuries to children in this community by over fifty percent.

It's so wonderful to be able to look at problems and start to solve them. It's very much like surgery, really. Figuring out how to solve problems, how to save lives, is a very surgical thing.

I don't have kids of my own. I would have loved to have had children. But if I had children, would I have had time to do all of this?

Maybe not.

I live in East Harlem. Spanish Harlem.

I like to open my windows and watch Harlem go by,

and it doesn't go by silently.

KEVIN TAYLOR

# Kevin Taylor, *36*

Harlem gives me sanctuary. But that sanctuary isn't about silence. Noise can be a sanctuary.

I live in East Harlem. Spanish Harlem. I like to open my windows and watch Harlem go by, and it doesn't go by silently. Sometimes, I turn my music off just to listen to the neighborhood: car horns honking, the bounce of a basketball, salsa pouring from a boom box, a girl yelling to a friend down the block. And Sunday mornings, it's perfectly still until noon. People are either getting ready for church or they're sleeping off a wild night. Those noises make living here pleasurable. My ear seeks those sounds because I grew up with them.

I'm from Washington, D.C. Chocolate City. I grew up in the Greenleaf projects. We only had three floors in our buildings and four apartments on each floor. There was a courtyard in the middle where kids played four square and hopscotch and kick ball. Mothers watched from benches.

The courtyard was always filled with noise. People would put speakers in the window on the weekend because the neighborhood was about music. And you know what, we understood that not everybody on the street had a stereo, so you didn't mind sharing. And nobody minded hearing the music blare. It wasn't no, "Turn that shit down!" And if the right record came on, you'd see kids do a little break dancing in the midst of their games. Or if the right oldie came on, your mother would jump up and she'd say, "Y'all don't know nuthin'. Come here, boy. Dance with your mama." You'd hide your face behind your hands but you'd peek between your fingers because you didn't know your mother could dance.

So many people try to create silence where they live. To me, that's a mausoleum. I want to live life and I want to *hear* life. If I didn't appreciate the sounds of Harlem, I'd live in Westchester.

There's a hip-hop dance called the Harlem Shake. I think it was introduced to the world through a video by Eve called "Who's That Girl?" Puff Daddy has the Harlem Shake in one of his videos, too. It's an indescribable dance. It's a lot of shoulders. It's a shimmy meets a break dance with a little Vogue thrown in—a dance only kids can do because it requires no vertebrae.

I remember shopping near 125th Street one day. Think I was on 127th and Adam Clayton Powell. I saw four or five boys hanging out on the corner. They were about thirteen or fourteen years old. The boys were leaning on a brown hooptie. That's what we used to call those big cars from the sixties: "Look at that old man driving that hooptie." Now, kids buy them for less than five hundred bucks just to get them and their buddies around. The hooptie's windows were down and the radio was booming. Just then, Puff Daddy's song came on and it was like something woke up in the boys. They began doing the Harlem Shake. No one said, "Hey, here's that song. Let's dance!" It just happened spontaneously. It was very much like they were saying, "We live in the hotbed of where this dance was created. It's ours. It's us." It was amazing to see.

Hearing the sounds of a neighborhood can be like that music, like the hip-hop those boys heard. It may not change your life, but it can make your day. And that's all music is supposed to do.

Harlem has been the dance capital

of the world for a long time.

ROBERT GARLAND

# Robert Garland, *40*

CHOREOGRAPHER AT DANCE THEATRE
OF HARLEM

One of my most popular ballets is called *New Bach*. It's set to Bach's Violin Concerto in A Minor. When I was working on it, I knew I wanted to create something different. I had done other ballets that were so grand. They had busy sets and colorful costumes and bright lights and billowing smoke. I said, "Enough! Now I'm going to simplify. I'm going to reduce it to what I like to do, to what I know."

Ever since Arthur Mitchell founded Dance Theatre of Harlem in 1969, it has opened the doors of classical ballet to African-American dancers. People of all races and ethnicities participate, but it is by and large an African-American organization and we've created a lot of ballets that have African- or African-American–based themes. I wanted to stay true to that mission. At the same time, I wanted to create something new and vibrant. I found what I was looking for while hanging out at a club in Harlem named Two-Minute Warning.

The club's music was hip-hop and loud. The crowd was full of energy. Suddenly, the music stopped and an amplified voice announced a Harlem Shake contest. Seemed to me that there were a lot of underaged kids in the club, but they were the ones who knew how to do the Harlem Shake. Their arms and shoulders twitched in fierce rhythm. It was incredible. It was a demonstration of what happens on the underbelly of this community. It wasn't about the familiar faces of Harlem you read about in the papers, like Congressman Charlie Rangel's Empowerment Zone or Al Sharpton running for president. This was the authentic face of Harlem expressing itself artistically on a dance floor. This was a moment uniquely American. So that night, I decided to put the Harlem Shake in my ballet.

The Harlem Shake grew out of Harlem. There's a famous basketball tournament in Harlem, an annual community tournament called the Rucker. All the stars from the NBA come and play alongside all the great "street" basketball players. During half-time, beginning back in the nineties, this guy named Al, Al something, would entertain the fans with his unique dance. Everyone looked forward to seeing it. They'd say, "Here comes Al doing that shaking thing." Everyone loved it. Summer students would come back and say, "Mr. Garland, you gotta go to the Rucker and see this guy dance at half-time. He's hysterical." It all started with Al at the the Rucker.

At the premiere of *New Bach*, the reaction to the Harlem Shake was bipolar. The traditional ballet audience probably would have missed it. But another section of the audience—mainly in the balcony, mind you—erupted when they saw it for that brief moment. All the papers talked about it. One of the dancers saw a review in the *Times* and he said, "Oh, my God! She called the Harlem Shake the Plié Wiggle, Plié Wiggle."

Not everybody thought I did such a great thing. But that's the beautiful thing about being American. We make those odd combinations and see what happens. Harlem has always been about that, about keeping American artistic expression vibrant and fresh.

The Harlem Shake is a dance of validation. It's a celebration of ourselves. Harlem has been the dance capital of the world for a long time.

My classmate said, "A Negro spiritual?

No one sings a Negro spiritual at a Juilliard audition."

I said, "Well, I am."

NOAH STEWART

# Noah Stewart, *22*

One day, on my lunch break, I walked into Mr. Lirtzman's office. Mr. Lirtzman taught music history when I was in the eleventh grade, and he made history fun. He was watching a laser disc. I heard this powerful voice singing opera, this incredible voice. I looked at the screen and saw a beautiful black woman. She had on a black, sleeveless gown with pearls. Her hair was up and she held her head high. She was singing Verdi's *Requiem* in Latin and she seemed to tower above the chorus and orchestra. She was singing from the heart. You can't teach that. Mr. Lirtzman said her name was Leontyne Price, a legendary soprano, a true diva. I had goose bumps. I said to Mr. Lirtzman, "I want to do that!"

I worked so hard at learning to sing opera. I came from nothing, but my mother always said, "Wealth isn't measured by money. It's measured by knowledge." I always felt I had to achieve because my mother gave me so much. A couple of years before I was born, she took a bus from New Orleans and moved to Harlem. She arrived on a Friday, found a job as a cashier that Saturday, and started work that Monday. She's had that same job for twenty-five years.

In my senior year, I heard that Leontyne Price was doing a CD signing at Tower Records. I got there two hours early and was the second person on line. A couple of hundred people showed up. I was so nervous when I spoke to her. I told her, "I want to be a professional opera singer and I'm trying out for Juilliard." She said, "Well, you probably know I went there. I think that's the best school for you." I said, "At the audition, I'm going to sing the spiritual I've heard you perform, 'Witness.' " She said, "That's not an ordinary song. Sing it from the heart." I felt like I had been blessed by the Pope.

I guess I was naive because I never understood the prestige of Juilliard. When I told people I was applying, they said. "Wow, that's the Harvard of the arts world!" An African-American classmate asked me what I was singing at the audition. I told her I was singing four pieces: "Where'er You Walk" by Handel; "Selve Amiche" by Caldara, which is in Italian; "Les Berceaux" by Fauré, which is in French; and "Witness," a Negro spiritual by Hall Johnson, an African American composer. My classmate said, "A Negro spiritual? No one sings a Negro spiritual at a Juilliard audition." I said, "Well, I am."

At the audition, eight instructors sat behind a long table. I was so nervous that I couldn't look at their eyes; I stared out the windows above their heads. I could see the sky. I was a little shaky at first, but I picked up steam. When I got to the last song, I thought about Leontyne Price, how she sang with such strength. I looked them in the eye and sang "Witness":

*Oh, Lord what manner of man is dis?*
*All nations in Him are blest;*
*All things are done by His will;*
*He spoke to de sea an' de sea stood still.*

When I finished I said, "Thank you," and walked toward the door. I could hear a buzz from the table. I knew I was in. The last thing Leontyne Price had said to me was, "Give 'em hell!"

I did.

Every Wednesday for the last three years,

I've sung the same song at a special service. . . . I've

never sang it the same way twice.

ALICE McCLARTY

# Alice McClarty, *65*

MEMBER OF THE SOUNDS OF GLORY CHOIR

At one time in my life, I drank, I gambled, I fornicated. And I won't lie to you. I loved it. Especially the fornicating. But your temple is supposed to be clean. Mine was unclean. So I gave those things up to live by the book. When I gave them up, my singing got better.

I sing every week at church in Harlem, but I grew up in New Orleans. My family attended Shiloh Baptist. My mother was the church organist, the church pianist, the church everything musical. Only thing she couldn't do well was sing. By the time she finished a song, she had sung all four parts: soprano, alto, tenor, and bass. And not intentionally. But I was born with the gift.

I started leading the choir when I was nine. When I sang, they'd be screaming and hollering and falling out. The ushers would fan people or carry them away. Back then, I sang from the head; now, I sing from the heart. That means that I don't have a set way to do a song anymore. I flow in the spirit. I sing with the anointing.

Every Wednesday for the last three years, I've sung the same song at a special service at Memorial Baptist. The song's called "He's Sweet I Know." I've never sang it the same way twice. The same song for three years, and God has given me a different version every week. That's the anointing.

I might sing the first half of the song at a slower tempo. Or I might add a few words to the lyrics. Or I might stress a different word. The song goes like this:

*He's sweet I know,*
*He's sweet I know.*
*Storm clouds may rise,*
*Strong winds may blow.*

One week I might say, "Hee-ee-ee-ee's *sweet*-I-knoo-oo-oo." The next week I might say, "Heeeeee's sweet I-*know*." The week after that I might say, "Storm clouds may rise—in my life. Strong winds may blow—*yes*, they do." You'd call it improvising if it came from the head. But it comes from the spirit.

About thirty years ago, I had several offers to sing the blues. They offered me recording contracts. They offered me a job in Las Vegas, making seven hundred dollars a week. When Carol Channing got sick, they offered me her part in *Hello, Dolly*. When I turned them down, they gave the job to Mahalia Jackson, the greatest gospel singer of our time.

Mahalia Jackson was from New Orleans, too. When her father died, I sang at his funeral. I was nineteen. She lived in Chicago at the time. I wanted to leave home so I moved to Chicago, too. I called her up after a week. She said, "I remember you! You sang that beautiful song. Where are you staying?" I said, "I'm staying at the Y." She said, "Girl, come on out that Y. Your mama wouldn't want you in no Y by yourself. Come on to my house." Mahalia Jackson treated me like family. She'd cook gumbo and invite all the big names in gospel: the Martin Singers, James Cleveland, everybody. I lived with her a year before I moved back home. I left because I couldn't find a job. The only thing I knew how to do was sing in church.

It's still the only thing I know how to do.

I went all around the world with my music

just to get back to what my mother used to tell me

as a boy: "Prayer changes all things."

LONNIE YOUNGBLOOD

# Lonnie Youngblood, *59*

When I was seven, I saw the great Louis Jordan play the saxophone on TV. I think it was the "Ed Sullivan Show." If you've ever heard of that Broadway musical called *Five Guys Named Moe*, well that was the Louis Jordan story. I remember the way the audience responded to him, the excitement. I may have lived in Augusta, Georgia, but that day, I knew the saxophone was for me.

For three years, I begged my parents for an alto saxophone. It cost $120.26. Might as well cost ten thousand dollars. But my father worked so hard to buy me that horn. After he bought it, he got angry when he found out he had to pay another two dollars per lesson.

My Uncle Earl was a boogie-woogie piano player. On Saturday nights, when I was eleven or twelve, he took me to the honky-tonk clubs to play with him. I could play only one riff: *Do-do-do, do-do-do, do, do, do-do-do*. People got a kick out it. They'd say, "He don't know much, but he knows *that*." My mother wasn't crazy about me going to the honky-tonks, but my father said, "I paid good money for that horn, I want to hear some music."

When I graduated from high school, I auditioned with a band in New Jersey, the Paul Farano Organ Trio. My mother had met a lady who sang in the band. The lady, Pearl Reeves, was telling my mother that their saxophone player had just quit. My mother said, "Well, you need to call my son. He's great!" The band sent me a ticket. I said, "Mama, you know I ain't ready to go up North." She said, "Just shut up and get ready." She said, "Prayer changes all things. Start praying!"

The band walked in the audition room and looked right past me. They said, "Where is he?" I said, "Here I am." Pearl Reeves said, "Oh my, he's just a baby!" That's why I changed my name. I was Lonnie Thomas, but I became Lonnie Youngblood.

I was working seven nights a week, making fifteen dollars a night. I'd never seen that much money. By my early twenties, I had made a name for myself, started my own band, and moved to Harlem. All the big names wanted me. I worked with Ben E. King, Sam and Dave, Joe Simon, James Brown, Jackie Wilson, on and on. I made records. I performed in Italy, Korea, Africa. If I haven't performed there, I've flown over it.

One day, a friend said, "You got to try this." He unfolded a hundred dollar bill, and a gram of cocaine was in the crease. I took a snort and became addicted for the next twenty years. I used all the time, no matter where I was or who I was with.

Drugs make you sink pretty low. I took cocaine with some people in Harlem once and a guy dropped dead. His heart exploded from snorting the same cocaine I was snorting. We just moved him to the side and kept on snorting.

I didn't want to live like that anymore. Twelve years ago, God delivered me from that addiction. Now, I play in a church band and on Saturdays I perform jazz at Sylvia's Restaurant on Lenox.

I went all around the world with my music just to get back to what my mother used to tell me as a boy: "Prayer changes all things."

Frank Schiffman owned the Apollo Theater.

He asked my brother and me if we wanted to move

our studio . . . next to the Apollo. But he wouldn't let us rent

the space on the street level—only the space one flight up.

Only whites were allowed space on the street level.

That's how it was on 125th Street. That's how it was in Harlem.


MARVIN SMITH

# Marvin Smith, *91*

PHOTOGRAPHER

Morgan, my twin brother, and I were born in 1910. Well, we were two country boys from Nicholasville, Kentucky. Our parents were sharecroppers. We lived on the farm, and the next-door neighbors were white. We got along with them. We just didn't mess around with those white teenage girls.

Morgan and I liked to draw. We taught ourselves when we were little by tracing pictures in Sears and Roebuck catalogs. We liked making art. When we were in high school, a photographer in Lexington gave us an old camera. A white man. We didn't have time to draw anymore so we would take pictures of our neighbors and friends.

Morgan and I moved to New York in 1933. Blacks had no place to go but Harlem. It was a place of opportunity. In 1940, my brother and I rented a space on 125th Street, where the state office building is now. That was our first studio. Frank Schiffman owned the Apollo Theater. He asked my brother and me if we wanted to move our studio to his building at 243 West 125th, next to the Apollo. But he wouldn't let us rent the space on the street level—only the space one flight up. Only whites were allowed space on the street level. That's how it was on 125th Street. That's how it was in Harlem.

Back then, *Life* magazine made my brother and me an offer. They wanted photos of Harlem, misery in Harlem. Very few blacks had assignments from major publications in those days. But we didn't want to take those kind of photos. There were so many negative pictures taken at the time: blacks killing blacks, blacks loitering in the streets. Morgan and I stayed away from that. Blacks were doing things in Harlem, positive things. We had doctors and lawyers and good families. Marvin and I took those kind of photos. Gordon Parks took the assignment from *Life* magazine. He was a dear friend of ours. We weren't angry at him because we weren't competing. Morgan and I were doing what we thought should be done and Gordon was doing what he wanted to do. And he did a good job.

Marvin and I photographed actors and actresses: Dorothy Dandridge, Lena Horne, Marlene Dietrich, Fredi Washington, Paul Robeson. We photographed most of the famous black athletes of the time: Jackie Robinson, who broke the color line in baseball; tennis great Althea Gibson, the first black to win at Wimbledon. Boxing champ Joe Louis was one of our best customers. We photographed leaders like Roy Wilkins, Mary McLeod Bethune, Father Divine, even First Lady Eleanor Roosevelt.

My favorite person to photograph was a black woman from Carolina. She was a famous photographer's model. She was beautiful. But she was advised to pass for Latin, which she could and did. She was the most exciting woman I worked with but I couldn't even talk about her because it would have spoiled her career.

When our photography book came out a few years ago, I saw Harry Belafonte at the Schomburg Center and he said, "Hey, I love your book. How come I wasn't in it?" I said, "You didn't come to our studio." It was simple as that. But he had no choice. Most black artists in that day were managed by white people, and the managers sent them to white photographers downtown.

I wish my brother was here to enjoy the glory our photographs receive. He died in 1993. People always want to know what pictures did I take and what pictures did Morgan take. It didn't matter to us as long as the picture came out. We were a team. Now he's gone. And I'm running out of time.

Hey, the House name has been on the window

for 'bout fifty years. You got to do more than cut heads.

DAVID HOUSE

BARBER Shop
1953
BOYS, BOYS
EVERY
WEDNESDAY
HAIRCUTS:
YES WE'RE
OPEN
jazzmobi
jazzmobi
jazzmobi
118TH STREET OLDTIMERS

# David House, 65

BARBERSHOP OWNER

$M$y father learned to cut heads in the war, World War II. When he came back to Harlem, he saw a vacant storefront on Seventh Avenue. A black dentist, a Jamaican, owned the building. That was unusual at that time. The dentist had a Jewish superintendent, who was married to a black woman. That was unusual, too. The super was in the dentist's office when my father went by. My father said, "I'd like to rent the storefront. I want to open a barbershop." The dentist said, "Sorry, I rented to a barber once and it didn't work out." But the super said, "Doctor, don't you know who this is?"

Coal furnaces were prevalent in those days. When winter was severe, you had to wait weeks for your coal supply. Sometimes you had to depend upon your neighbor to see you through. Well, my grandfather, Mali House, was the super at a building across the avenue. So the dentist's super said, "This is Mr. House's son. Mr. House, the one who loans us coal." The dentist said, "Oh, yeah? Sure, you got the place."

My father opened this barbershop in January of 1946. I was ten years old. There were three barbers beside himself. Listen, some interesting people have sat in these old chairs. Malcolm X even came in once. Think it was 1961. He got a manicure from Sister Dorothy. She was a member of the mosque. Men got manicures in those days. They wore pretty clothes, ran sweet hos, and walked on tiptoes.

Not long after the shop opened, this tall, elderly fellow came in. He asked my father, he said, "Barber, are you working?" My father said, "Yeah." The man took off his hat and said, "Good, 'cause I want my head shaved clean as mama's chitlins." Everybody laughed.

The man and my father started talking about down South. The man said, "Even if we bleached our skin and rolled in powder, those crackers still wouldn't give us a break." When the man left, another customer said, "Oh, so you working on the champ now?" My father said, "Champ? What champ?" The customer said, "That was Jack Johnson who just walked out." Jack Johnson was the first black heavyweight champ of the world, beat all the white boxers in his day. White people hated Jack Johnson. Too proud. Afraid of nobody. Plus, he married a white woman. Jack Johnson died in a car accident in North Carolina later that year. They say a white hospital could have saved his life, but they wouldn't give him blood.

And when I was about fifteen, Charlie "Bird" Parker came in for a haircut. A jazz legend. Played the sax. He sat in Slim's chair. Later on, Slim would teach me to cut heads because my father was impatient with me. I was slow when it came to learning new things. Slim was an alcoholic, but he had patience. Okay, Charlie Parker.

I brushed Charlie Parker off when Slim finished. I shined shoes and brushed customers off. Charlie Parker said, "Wait, wait, junior. You don't have to do that." He gave me a tip then he said, "Junior, promise me you'll never use dope. Promise me!" I was shocked but I said, "I promise." Charlie Parker was addicted to heroin, you know.

I try to give young men a message, too. When a kid gets out of my chair, I tell him, "Stay away from drugs!" I yell it so it gives him a jolt. "Go to school! You're our next doctor, our next mayor. We need you, young man!" Hey, the House name has been on the window for 'bout fifty years. You got to do more than cut heads.

[Author's update: David House retired and closed shop in November 2002.]

Our order, the Franciscan Handmaids,

was founded in 1916. Someone made the remark back then,

"You can dress them up like nuns, but you can't stop them

from stealing chickens."

SISTER LORETTA THERESA RICHARDS

# Sister Loretta Theresa Richards, FHM, *72*

I was a junior in high school when I realized I wanted to be a nun. My friend Mary went to Hunter High School and she invited me to a party. I was dancing with a young man from Hunter. He said, "What school do you go to?" I said, "I go to Cathedral." He looked at me and said, "Cathedral? Do you want to be a nun?" I said, "Of course not!" We kept dancing. But right after the words came out of my mouth I said to myself, *You're lying. You do want to be a nun.*

So I said, *I guess I should let my mother in on this.* I decided to write her a letter. A letter, right. We lived in a tiny apartment but I wrote her a letter. It said something like: "Dear Mother: I would like to enter the convent. But I will delay it for one year. I want to give you time to adjust."

That night, I heard my mother talking to my older sister, Alice, at the kitchen table. In black families, everything happens at the kitchen table. That's where your mother does your hair. That's where you do your homework. We even ate at the kitchen table, imagine that. They thought I was asleep, but I heard my mother say to Alice, "Your sister wants to become a sister." I could tell by the tone of her voice that she wasn't opposed to it. But my mother never talked to me about it. Not once.

I've been a nun since 1948. At that time, white congregations were not accepting of blacks. Our order, the Franciscan Handmaids, was founded in 1916. Someone made the remark back then, "You can dress them up like nuns, but you can't stop them from stealing chickens."

Do I miss having a family of my own? I'm a teacher. The children I've taught *are* my children. I remember the first child I taught who died. Maurice. He died young, in his twenties. He was in my first seventh-grade class. A sweet boy. I still remember looking at that casket and feeling such an emptiness. I thought, *My God, if I feel this bad how must his mother feel?*

Children are a blessing. It infuriates me when I walk through Marcus Garvey Park and I hear parents cursing at their children. I remember hearing this woman using the most offensive language to a child in a stroller. I didn't say anything to the woman, I just looked. She started cursing me and telling me, "This is *my* child and ain't *nobody* gonna tell me how to raise up my child." We have to pray for ourselves, that we're not violent in our speech or our actions.

I was on my way to an appointment with my eye doctor one day. When I walked through the parlor of our convent, one of the sisters gasped at the television. She said, "A second plane just crashed into the World Trade Center." I said, "No, it didn't," and I proceeded out the door. It was so terrible that I was telling her she wasn't seeing what she was seeing. So terrible.

But, yes, we have to pray for terrorists, too. The Lord prayed from the cross, "Father, forgive them for they know not what they do." I just have to bring it back to myself. How, in little ways, do I do the unbelievable, the unthinkable, the unkind? I can't do anything about what they do out there. I can only do something about me. And if we all did that, it could change the world.

My friend Floyd ran into the class on September 11th.

"They bombed the World Trade Center!"

KAREEM SENATUS

# Kareem Senatus, *17*

HIGH SCHOOL STUDENT

I go to Rice High School in Harlem. Rice is a Catholic school for boys. It's an old-fashioned school with old-fashioned values. Some people used to put it down because it's in Harlem. They used to say, "Rice is the public school of all Catholic schools." But that's changing now. We're stronger in academics.

My friend Floyd ran into the class on September 11th. "They bombed the World Trade Center!" We said, "What?" He said, "Yeah, they said it on the radio." Everybody was in shock.

Parents came to pick up their children 'cause people were speculating that the terrorists might crash planes into government buildings, and the state office building, the Adam Clayton Powell building, is on 125th, just a block or two from the school. The kids said, "Oh, man! Let's go up to the Bronx. Ain't nothing up there but Yankee Stadium."

Later that day, I saw this lady crying on TV. She was near Ground Zero, holding a picture of her husband. Then it was no longer TV; I was actually there at the World Trade Center. I've felt what they were feeling—the tears, the sorrow, the feeling that something inside of you is wrong and it's going to break you apart. It's a real hard feeling to deal with.

When I was nine, my brother Naheem held me hostage. He had an argument with my sister one morning. He and Nakie, they were always fighting. Naheem wanted to come back in the house to change his school clothes or something, and Nakie wouldn't let him. He banged on the door. *Knock, knock, knock, knock, knock.* He rang the bell. *Ring, ring, ring, ring,*

*ring.* But Nakie wouldn't let him in. Naheem said, "All right, Kareem's not going to school." I said, "What you mean I'm not going to school?" He said, "You not going to school."

Our neighbor, Mrs. Brown, hears everything. Everybody's got that older neighbor who's like your grandmother. Eyes in back of her head. That's Mrs. Brown. Mrs. Brown said, "Now, Nakie, give Naheem his stuff so they can go to school." My sister gave in, and Naheem laughed at how she rolled her eyes. I started laughing, too. Naheem and I just laughed and laughed. We were real tight.

Naheem used to cut school a lot. He became engulfed in the streets. My moms laid the law down. She said, "Look, you gotta do what you gotta do to get your diploma."

About four o'clock one afternoon, we heard this banging and ringing at the door. My moms was washing dishes. I said, "That's Naheem," because that's how he knocked: *Knock, knock, knock, knock, knock. Ring, ring, ring, ring, ring.* But it wasn't Naheem. It was one of his friends, this guy named Da-Da. Da-Da's face was all red. He was crying. He said, "Yo, yo! Naheem got killed. Yo, Mrs. Senatus, Naheem got killed."

We think somebody was chasing Naheem home from school and he ran into a building and got cornered. He was shot once in the back of the head and twice in the back. He was a block from home.

When you go to a funeral and you see the body laying there and it doesn't look like your brother because there's no blood in the body, that's when you know he's dead and he'll always be dead. People should think about that before they go about their violent ways. People really need to calm it down. Find another way. Murder is senseless.

So I met Langston. He had an apartment

on 127th Street. He was very down to earth, just

an ordinary guy even though he was famous, the best known

writer of the Harlem Renaissance.

DOROTHY GOODE

# Dorothy Goode, *84*

BOARD MEMBER OF HARLEM YMCA

When I was in my early twenties, I edited Langston Hughes's first book on Jesse B. Simple. It was named *Simple Speaks His Mind*. The character of Simple was an uneducated working man from Harlem. He always had something to say about politics and race and his aching feet. My neighbor, Mr. Hugh Smythe, was supposed to edit the book, but he was an ambassador and got called away to go abroad and he asked if I would edit the book for Langston. I didn't know what the book was about so I said yes.

So I met Langston. He had an apartment on 127th Street. He was very down to earth, just an ordinary guy even though he was famous, the best known writer of the Harlem Renaissance. He asked me what I thought of the book after I read it. I told him I didn't like it. I told him I didn't approve of the dialect his characters used. They sounded ignorant. I thought he should change all those "ain'ts" and "gonnas." Subjects and verbs didn't agree. I said, "I don't like that kind of talk, all that Harlemese." Langston said, "Well, that's how they talk in Harlem and that's how I'm going to write it." So I did the so-called editing his way. I got sixteen dollars for it.

Langston Hughes hung around Lenox Avenue and the YMCA on 135th Street, picking up the dialect from the people for his books. Back then, people didn't just go to the Y for recreation. When blacks came up from the South, they stayed with family or friends or they rented rooms at the Y until they could get on their feet. And when black celebrities came from out of town, they stayed at the Y: politicians, actors, writers like Ralph Ellison.

There was a lot of political activity at the Y. I was in a club called the Modern Trend, which was a mostly young people's club for the so-called intellectuals, the young people who were going to college and doing things: being activists, fighting for causes like jobs. We'd march in the streets and make speeches. Adam Clayton Powell Jr. was in that group, too. Adam became a congressman later on. He looked white and he married a woman who looked white, but they didn't try to pass.

People don't realize all the fights we had to fight. People talk about the South, but many stores in *Harlem* wouldn't hire blacks. You could be highly educated but whites still treated you like a shoeshine boy. We had teachers who came up from the South, good teachers, who had to work as subs for years because they wouldn't give them accreditation. It was really tough for men. A lot of young black doctors and lawyers started out as redcaps and Pullman porters at Pennsylvania Station. The redcaps would carry your luggage to the train, and the porters worked on the train, helping you into your sleeping car and such. Menial jobs. They struggled. People say, "But look at all the accomplishments blacks have made." Yeah, but nobody gave us those. We had to fight for them.

You learned to take insults in stride because you knew they were going to happen. Like if I was standing next to a dark-skinned girl at my job in the Housing Department, people in the office would say, "Oh, you two look just alike." So I would go around to all the Italians and Jews and call them each other's names. I'd call Frank "David," I'd call David "Frank." They'd say, "What's wrong with you?" I said, "Oh, well, you all look alike." So that cut that out. For blacks back in my day, life was a chain of little insults. And some weren't so little.

You know, when people used to ask

where I lived, I'd say, "Upper Manhattan." But I'm not

ashamed anymore. I shout "Harlem" from the mountains.


ALVIN REED

# Alvin Reed, *62*

OWNER OF LENOX LOUNGE

When I was in the third or fourth grade, this white man came into our apartment. He had curly hair, sandy-colored. He wore a shirt and tie. No jacket. I don't remember what day of the week it was, but it was evening time. We had just finished dinner. When he came inside, the man said something to my mother and my mother said, "Y'all go in the kitchen." She was talking to me, my sister, Delores, who was two years older than me, and my brother, Wallace, two years younger than me.

My family lived in a railroad flat apartment at 121 West 133rd Street. A railroad flat, that's an apartment with all the rooms lined up and open. If you had the back room, you had to walk through everybody's room to get to yours. There was no privacy. I don't know how my parents ever had sex.

The man had us sit at the kitchen table. He kept looking at us and tilting his head. He saw a loaf of bread and got a slice. Now, to us, bread was precious. We didn't eat meat sandwiches for lunch. We had mayonnaise sandwiches or sugar sandwiches or just plain bread. Sometimes we didn't even have sandwiches. We had sweet water: Put some sugar in a glass of water and stir it up. When we didn't have any food, my mother would send us next door to borrow rice and beans or something.

The white man took that slice of bread and tore it into three pieces. He gave me a piece, my brother a piece, and my sister a piece. Then he pulled out a camera and took our picture. Took our picture.

Some time later, can't remember how long, a bunch of kids were huddled around at school, looking at something. I came to see what it was. It was a picture of me, Delores, and Wallace in a magazine. It was *Look* magazine or *Life* or *Awake*. Can't remember. The three of us were holding a piece of bread in our hands. The picture took up the whole page. But I didn't see it long because I took off running. One boy was saying, "Bus-ter's poor, Bus-ter's poor." Buster was my nickname.

In those days, when people were on welfare it was a secret. They were ashamed. But the thing is, we *weren't* on welfare. My father had a good job so we couldn't qualify for welfare, but we were poor because my father didn't bring his money home. He was a country boy, and Harlem gamblers would out-slick him. Cards, dice, playing the numbers. They'd say, "Hey, don't start the game 'til Richard gets here." My father never came home on payday. We wouldn't see him for two or three days, until all the money was gone. He'd say something like, "I got robbed."

My mother was a maid. We survived on her salary, which wasn't much. Her dream was to get a place in the projects, leave our railroad flat to the rats and roaches. I think my mother thought the magazine photo was going to bring attention to our plight so we could move into the projects. Didn't happen.

You know, when people used to ask where I lived, I'd say, "Upper Manhattan." But I'm not ashamed anymore. I shout "Harlem" from the mountains.

If you gotta die, and we all gotta die,

it's me you want to bury you. Everybody in Harlem knows that.

I'm the guy who puts the smile on your face. Other places,

you just look dead.

ISAIAH OWENS

# Isaiah Owens, 50

## FUNERAL HOME OWNER

If you gotta die, and we all gotta die, it's me you want to bury you. Everybody in Harlem knows that. I'm the guy who puts the smile on your face. Other places, you just look dead.

I'm gonna look sharp at your funeral, too. I wear tails and a top hat because a man can't get any more dressed up than that. It's the ultimate in dress, which shows the ultimate respect for the departed.

I came out my mother's womb a funeral director. A toy to other kids was an old car tire or a hubcap. They'd roll it and roll it and pretend that it was a school bus or a truck. While the other kids were doing that, I was across the way having a funeral.

At five years old, I was holding funerals for little creatures, frogs and things. I'd preach a sermon and sing gospel like it was a real funeral. Grown-ups would say, "That boy will bury anything that goes hippy-hopping through the yard." But that's why I'm the best in Harlem. Lots of practice.

I grew up in Branchville, South Carolina. Small town. Too small for a stoplight. In the black community back then, when you died they put your body on a cooling board in the house. Later on they'd put you in a box and bury you. Not a casket, a box.

My grandfather was planning to open a funeral home and start building caskets so people could have a decent burial. But he got killed in 1947. When I came along in 1950, they say his dreams were in me. And sure enough, I moved to New York and started my own funeral home when I was twenty. My uncles and them used to say I was their father all over again. His name was Isaiah, just like mine.

My cousin, Lizzy Ruth, who is ninety-two, told me one day about her great-grandmother, who had been a slave. Her great-grandmother told her about how the slaves had to pick so much cotton in a day. If they didn't, the massa would strip their clothes off— the men and the women—tie them to a tree, and whip them 'til blood ran like water. One time, a man screamed out, "Massa, can I have a tater?" He was hungry. Bleeding to death and hungry. When she told me that, I got teary.

Lizzy Ruth said if a slave died, they'd have only thirty minutes to bury them. When they went down in the woods for the burial, they'd sing songs like:

*When all God's Children get together,*
*What a time, what a time!*
*We're going to sit down on the banks of the river,*
*And what a time, what a time, what a time!*

That song works you. I sang that one when we buried Herbert Woods, Sylvia's husband. In Harlem, they always ask me to sing those old songs at funerals. Know 'em all. But funny thing is that I don't think I can sing. I *know* I can't sing. But I sing anyhow because I don't want the old songs to die.

In 1960, Cuba's Fidel Castro stayed at the Hotel Theresa,

and Russian premier Nikita Khrushchev came to visit him. . . . I got

a room on the same floor as Castro. . . . One day, I came out of

my room and there were dozens of chickens in the hallway.

Live chickens, running and clucking.

EVELYN CUNNINGHAM

# Evelyn Cunningham, *85*

$M$y friends extend from activist Al Sharpton to philanthropist Brooke Astor. That's what a career in journalism has done for me. My first job was in the Harlem office of the *Pittsburgh Courier*. The *Courier* was the largest black newspaper in the world. It had fourteen editions. The Harlem editor was courting my aunt, so I didn't get the job legitimately. But I made it clear that I was not going to do the society beat, covering weddings and fashion shows. My heart has always been with hard news.

The *Courier* office was directly across the street from the Hotel Theresa, which was the hub of black life. Ron Brown, who was President Clinton's Commerce Secretary when he was killed in a plane crash, grew up in the hotel. His father, Bill Brown, was the manager.

Celebrities had this need to stand in front of the hotel. Joe Louis, the boxer, claimed not to like the attention, but he always signed autographs in front of the hotel for hours. I bumped into Duke Ellington several times in the lobby. He'd say, "How is my doll today? You're looking so beautiful." As a reporter, I should have asked him who he was visiting, but he always got me so flustered. I also saw A. Philip Randolph, who organized the Brotherhood of Sleeping Car Porters union. Malcolm X always spoke catty-cornered to the Hotel Theresa. He was usually on a ladder, surrounded by his followers. Gordon Parks, the famous photographer, I first met him at the hotel's bar. We're friends to this day. We both have white hair now, and we spend a lot of time going, "Huh, what did you say?"

In 1960, Cuba's Fidel Castro stayed at the Hotel Theresa, and Russian premier Nikita

Khrushchev came to visit him. That was front-page news across the world. They were in town for a meeting at the United Nations. I got a room on the same floor as Castro, and I ran up and down the hallway, with a pencil and paper, hoping to get an interview. One day, I came out of my room and there were dozens of chickens in the hallway. Live chickens, running and clucking. Castro's people had brought them from Cuba for him to eat. I interviewed Castro in the hallway for a brief moment before his guards rushed him along.

During the Civil Rights Movement, I begged to be reassigned to one of the offices down South, in Birmingham or Montgomery. All of the male reporters had been run out of town so they finally said, "Oh, okay, let's send Cunningham."

I was checking into a seedy hotel in Montgomery that was half a block from Dr. Martin Luther King's home when I heard an explosion. The clerk said, "Oh, my God! That's Dr. King's house." I rushed over there. Before long, about a hundred black people gathered in his front lawn, holding pipes, empty Coke bottles, and stones. They were ready to go out and kill whoever had done this.

Dr. King came out and assured the crowd that his wife and kids were safe in the back of the house. And then he talked. I mean he *talked*. He said that answering violence with violence was not God's way. You don't need those weapons in your hands, he said. We have the weapon of courage. We have the weapon of brotherhood. We have the weapon of righteousness. As he spoke, I heard these thudding sounds all around me. It was the bottles and pipes and stones falling to the ground. I stood there and cried. That was the first time I ever saw Dr. King. And that was the first story I wrote about the movement.

I think it's like the end of your childhood

when they destroy something that was so special to you. It's like

what they did to the Audubon Ballroom, where Malcolm X

was assassinated. That is sacred ground, but now it's a retail space.

My nickname for Harlem is "Harm Them."


TONY MEDINA

# Tony Medina, 35

POET

My father was born in Harlem, the first of nine. He had a brother named Ralph, the second born. One hot, hot summer night, Uncle Ralph went out to sleep on the fire escape of their tenement. It was cooler out there. That night, while Uncle Ralph slept, the fire escape collapsed and Uncle Ralph died. That building, where my father grew up, where his brother died, is still there on 118th Street and Park.

There's this big rock next to the building, a boulder that juts from the earth like a hill. It was too big to remove so developers just built around it. That rock was where all the kids in my father's neighborhood played. My father said the whole block was like a family, and all the kids in the neighborhood—the black kids, the Puerto Rican kids—would climb the rock and chase each other around it. It was a central part of their imagination. I can imagine my father and Uncle Ralph looking up at that big rock and saying, "We're superheroes! Let's climb this mountain!" There had to be many a kid who fell off that rock and busted his butt. When you grow up poor, you turn an abandoned mattress into a makeshift trampoline, and you make believe that a stubborn rock is a mighty mountain, and you sleep out on the shoddy fire escape because there's no air conditioner.

My father's parents came from Puerto Rico and met in Harlem. His mother was a black Puerto Rican and his father was a white Puerto Rican. That's what Puerto Ricans are, a mixture of everybody. The hospital put "Negro" on my father's birth certificate because his skin was a rich, dark brown. As far as they were concerned, "We define you by how you look not where you're from, not your culture, so, *bam*, you're black—not a black Puerto Rican."

My father watched his neighborhood go through so many transformations. First, the white people started jetting—the Jews and Italians. My father was a shoe-shine boy when heroin started ravaging Harlem. He shined the shoes of a savvy hustler named Detroit Red, who later transformed himself and became Malcolm X. Hustlers were celebrities back then. My father would hang out with them and hear Billie Holiday and John Coltrane. My father was tight with Nicky Barnes, the infamous Harlem drug dealer. He knew all those cats and he ended up doing time for drugs himself, but he turned his life around and became a drug rehab counselor.

Later, my father saw 116th Street divide. The west side became African—Senegal, Nigeria, Somalia. And the east side, which for the last forty years or more was Puerto Rican and Italian, it became populated by Mexican and South American immigrants. And then my father saw the white folks coming back to Harlem. Now they're tearing down these grand, prewar buildings and replacing them with these stiff, boring, so-called modern buildings. My father said they were destroying the whole face of Harlem.

My father just died. He was living in an old-folks' home on 121st and Lexington, not far from where he grew up. He lived to see them begin renovating his old neighborhood. They're going to tear down the tenement where my father grew up and where Uncle Ralph died, and they're blasting that old rock away. I think it's like the end of your childhood when they destroy something that was so special to you. It's like what they did to the Audubon Ballroom, where Malcolm X was assassinated. That is sacred ground, but now it's a retail space. My nickname for Harlem is "Harm Them."

When my wife and I bought our brownstone

in 1992, some of our friends said moving to Harlem was

"admirable." That was as positive as it got, "admirable," like we were

missionaries going to a Third World country.

PHILLIP ISOM

# Phillip Isom, *37, and wife Anne, with daughter*
*Aiyanna and son Phillip VI*

LAW FIRM PARTNER

When my wife and I bought our brownstone in 1992, some of our friends said moving to Harlem was "admirable." That was as positive as it got, "admirable," like we were missionaries going to a Third World country. Most of our friends bought houses in Westchester or the suburbs of New Jersey. They thought it made no sense at all: Two young people, graduates of Columbia's law school, who could live anywhere they wanted, were making a home in Harlem.

We heard all kinds of questions: "How long are you going to stay there? Do you really want to raise kids there? Will you feel safe there?" But here we are, nine years later, and now everyone wants to move here. Our friends say, "Wow, you guys were really pioneers!" But I don't see it that way. It was just always something I wanted to do. We weren't just moving to Harlem: We were moving to Strivers Row.

My mother and father always talked about Strivers Row. They thought the brownstones were beautiful, and they admired the African Americans who achieved success and lived there in the 1920s and 1930s: the judges, the lawyers, the doctors. Dr. Louis Wright, the surgeon who headed Harlem Hospital, lived on Strivers Row. Eubie Blake, the famous pianist and songwriter, lived here. And Vertner Tandy, the first African American to become a licensed architect in the state. That's why it's called Strivers Row, because the people who lived here were the achievers, the "strivers."

I grew up a world away from Strivers Row, in the projects near 110th and Park. That's considered East Harlem, also referred to as Spanish Harlem or El Barrio. It was fifty-fifty African American and Hispanic, mostly Puerto Rican but some Dominican. There was rivalry between black kids and Hispanic kids, but nothing too serious. They called us out of our names: *"morenos," "cocolos."* We just called them Puerto Ricans. "You Puerto Ricans this, you Puerto Ricans that." I didn't realize until I got older that all Hispanic people are not Puerto Rican.

It wasn't unusual for kids I knew to spend time in jail for drugs and violence. When I was fifteen, a friend of mine was shot in the head and killed by another kid who grew up in the building. My parents raised three boys in that environment and none of us got into trouble. My parents were saddened about how Harlem had fallen. But they talked a lot about the greatness of Harlem, especially Strivers Row.

Strivers Row is actually two different streets: 138th and 139th between Seventh and Eighth. I would come up here and admire the brownstones because they were so distinctive: the yellow brick, the paths between some of the houses, put there so that the original occupants could walk horses from the street to the rear alleys. The fact that trash is picked up in the rear is totally different from most of the brownstones in New York, and it makes the neighborhood look clean. Also, the houses have a uniform look. Throughout Harlem, you'll see only two or three brownstones on any given block that look alike. That's because they were typically built by different architects. But the homes on Strivers Row look alike because the developers had the resources to construct a whole block of buildings at a time.

As I grew up in the seventies, Harlem was a place that people wanted to escape. I never felt that way. I felt proud to be part of Harlem. That feeling must have come from the way my parents talked about it. I was never made to think that Harlem was a ghetto. Harlem is not a ghetto.

CRAIG MARBERRY conducted the interviews and wrote the essays that appear in *Spirit of Harlem*. He is a former television reporter and has written articles for the *Washington Post, Essence,* and the Harlem-based newspaper the *Amsterdam News.* Marberry is currently writing his next book, *Cuttin' Up: Wit and Wisdom in Black Barbershops.* He lives in Greensboro, North Carolina.

MICHAEL CUNNINGHAM is the photographer of *Spirit of Harlem.* He is the owner of Michael Cunningham Photography and the Executive Director of Urban Shutterbugs, a national nonprofit organization teaching photography to youth. He lives in Washington, D.C.

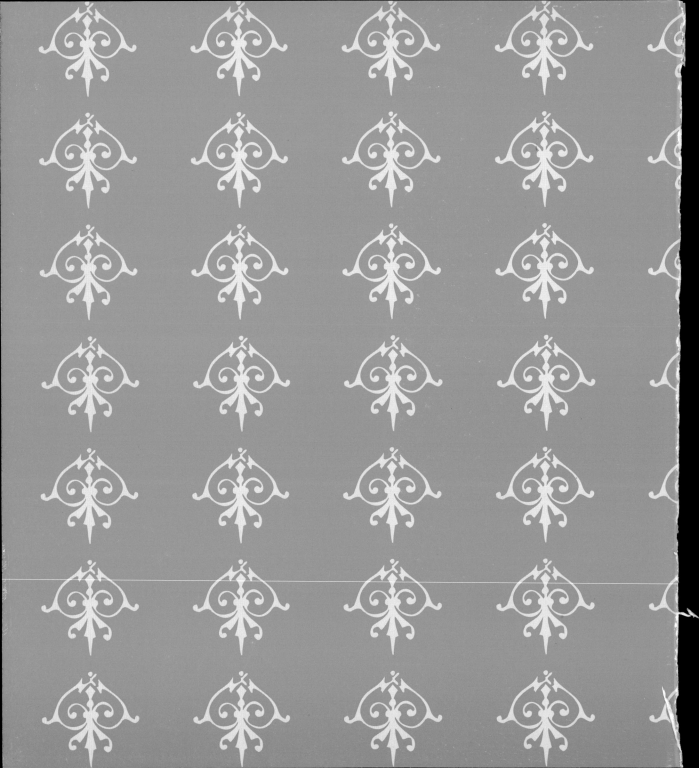